Success

as an

Adult Internet

Model

By
Antonio Giancarlo
Perfetti
("Tony Perfect")
With
Scott Gardner

Success as an Adult Internet Model
© 2008
Agile' Marketing Services
151 North 2nd Street
Fulton NY   13069

Published by
Dark Raptor Press

By "Tony Perfect" with Scott Gardner

www.AdultInternetModeling.com

Also available:

Adult Internet Modeling Workbook

SAIM™ and
SAIM 9 Rules™
Trademark of Agile' Marketing Services

Contents

HOW TO USE THIS BOOK

This isn't a library book you need to keep neat and clean for the next person. You should be reading this book with a highlighter in your hand. The margins are big enough for you to jot notes next to the text. If you need more room, there is plenty of blank space at the end of most of the chapters to write down your thoughts and ideas. Mark it up, then read the book again.

You can read the book from front to back, but don't be afraid to just jump to a particular chapter if it catches your eye.

There's also an associated web site where you can go and interact with the authors, as well as with other models. Ask questions, give suggestions, or just hang out and relax.

Most important, don't leave this book on a shelf somewhere. Take it with you when you go to shoots. Re-reading the SAIM 9 Rules™ doesn't hurt, and you might use your notes for ideas that can make a good shoot into a great one.

The authors wish you fun and success!

Take Note!

You'll see boxes like this on some pages. They contain important "extras" to the text.

Keep an eye out for them.

DON'T DO IT

This may seem crazy, but I'm going to start this book by trying to talk you out of becoming an adult Internet model. I have the same conversation with all the first-time model prospects I meet with.

Let's be honest, if I can talk you out of it, I (and other producers) don't have to deal with the problems shooting newcomers may eventually bring back to us. We have a lot fewer headaches if you walk into this with your eyes open and your mind straight. In the several years I've been producing content for the 'net, I've had models come back and beg me to retrieve their pictures or hide their faces. Only once have I been physically attacked, and those of us who produce content in a professional manner really don't need that.

Once we go over all the reasons not to do this, if you still want to become an adult model, you'll find a financially and artistically rewarding career. You can do it part-time or full-time, just once or over and over. You can make cash and wind up with some stunning photos for your portfolio. You'll meet lots of interesting people who are, counter to the stereotype, quite intelligent and articulate. You can take paid vacations almost anywhere you want to.

But before we get to that, let me burst your bubble.

Your relatives will see your work at some point. It may be your grandma surfing at the senior center, your child searching your nightstand for a bandage, or your dad opening an e-mail sent by one of your angry ex-lovers. Your friends will stop talking when you come into a room. Total strangers will see you on the street and say inappropriate things in front of the person you're with.

Once those pictures of you are out there, you're going to look back on some or all of them and wish you were heavier or lighter, had a different haircut, didn't have pimples on all those private places, or hadn't been wearing something that made you look stupid.

The fast cash will become addictive, almost like a drug. Want a new car? You'll start thinking in terms of hours spent in front of the camera.

Depending on the content, you could buy a new car after only a weekend spent on the set. You'll wind up begging people you've worked with for more shoots, and annoy the hell out of them. You might start bending your own limitations, and wind up sorry.

The business of adult modeling is a lot more work than 99% of the new-comers think. Taking off your clothes is the easy part. You have to negoti-ate your rates, get up early and go to bed late, deal with the same questions over and over again without snapping, and take physical and emotional rejection as a part of doing business.

Speaking of physical rejection, this is a tremendously shallow business. It's all about your "look." You'll get turned down because of your weight or lack of it, your hair color, hair length, your height, or your facial expression. Your teeth will be too crooked, too straight, or your ears lopsided. And you'll be told all this in the most unsympathetic terms by some of the ugli-est, nastiest specimens of humanity you'll ever want to meet. They'll ask you to take off your clothes, looking you over while they eat a liverwurst and onion sandwich. Scratching their prominent ass-crack, they'll tell you they can't hide your stretch marks, so they can't use you. All of this after you've traveled 100 miles on your own dime to get on location an hour before the shoot is scheduled to begin.

You'll be asked to wear clothes that were last washed who knows when. You'll be given toys and props that smell funky from old bodily secretions. Rugs will be dirty, beds will have bugs, rooms will be too cold or too hot.

You'll be expected to work with people who don't understand the basics of personal hygiene. Who think that covering sores with make-up makes them appealing again. Who think that a five minute break means it's time to snort, smoke and/or drink as much as possible, and then come back reeking of drugs, booze, vomit or just body funk. All the while, you're sup-posed to act like this is the best time you've ever had in your entire life, and that you're in a continual state of ecstasy.

As they say in business school, there is a "low barrier to entry" to the adult industry on both sides of the camera. That means, in short, "It doesn't take a rocket scientist to do this." You'll find the entry-level ranks of Internet modeling lacking in smarts and sanity, and populated by cheap hustlers and easy marks.

4

Still reading? Okay, I've made you suffer enough. It gets better from here.

In the following pages, you'll be introduced to the SAIM 9 Rules™. Follow these, and in just a few shoots you'll leave the rank and file behind. You'll be well on your way to making it to the top of the heap.

DEFINITIONS

SUCCESS

The definition of "success" is subjective – it's meaning changes from person to person. You can make lots of money. You can provide a good living for yourself and your family, pay off debts and buy the toys you always wanted.

You can also become recognized for your hard work and talent, make a name for yourself. Many Internet-based models develop a loyal fan base, following the model's career from site to site, and job to job.

Part-time modeling work can make you as much or more money than a regular full-time job, leaving you with plenty of time to spend with your family, to attend school, or to work on a hobby.

Being paid to travel the country, or even the world, is a perk many models enjoy.

Almost any definition of success is achievable with consistent, professional work in this industry.

ADULT CONTENT

"Adult" does not have to mean "porn," although porn certainly fits in there. For this book, our definition of "adult content" is anything where the intended audience is at or above the age of majority. As an example, content featuring models smoking cigarettes and cigars may have no nudity whatsoever, but the images are definitely geared towards adults.

Another aspect is that either implicitly or explicitly, pornographic and erotic content is meant to excite a sexual response from the viewer. The desired reaction could be anywhere between titillation and outright lust, or simply to shock the viewer. However, some type of reaction is expected.

Off the top of my head, and in no particular order within the categories, the following are some niches where adult content models can find work.

The lists are far from conclusive – I'm sure I've left out any number of niches.

Non-Nude	Nude	Fetish
Fashion	Art	S&M
Swimwear	Glamour	B&D
Lingerie	Figure	Leather/vinyl
Parts modeling	Erotic	Role play
Presentation/Spokesmodel	Implied	Cat fight
Automotive	Soft core	Goth
Alcohol	Hard core	Extreme
Tobacco		Shoes/feet
Pharmaceuticals		Smoking
Supplements		Age
Catalog		Race
Horror/Violence		Hair color
Fitness/Sport		Weight
		Uniforms/costumes
		Balloons
		Crush
		Tickling

INTERNET

The Internet is now where a majority of the jobs are, where the producers look for models, and where consumers look for content. If you're looking for a good paying adult modeling job, this is where you need to be.

The Internet has become a serious commercial presence. In the United States, it has drastically redefined – almost killed – the magazine industry.

Magazines target a defined interest group: car enthusiasts, business owners, men who want to see naked women. Because of the cost of producing and distributing a printed version of a periodical, magazines cannot have too narrow a focus. Sure, with the advent of more economical printing technologies, smaller content niches ("Exotic Car Bikini Babes") can be produced, but the cost of finding consumers and getting the magazine to them is still prohibitive.

The Internet, which consists loosely of e-mail, web sites and the rapidly-dwindling news groups, totally offloads any printing costs from the publisher to the consumer. Even the most expensive 'net distribution technologies (not the production costs, but things like software, web hosting and access fees) cost far less per month than even the cheapest way to print and distribute a paper magazine.

Because of that, niche and micro-niche publications are not only possible, but often more profitable than general interest sites.

What about appearing in stills and video advertising media? Billboards and TV commercials, for instance. With viewers turning away from traditional media, many of those adverts are being placed on the 'net. Advertisers are not constrained to purchasing X number of 30-second blocks. Many 'net videos are getting longer, and are produced more like short movies or TV shows.

Ads where stills are used are also increasingly interactive, resizing as mouse pointers move over them, or jumping out from the screen corners between pages. Even if your images do appear on TV or in a print publication, a version of the ad is probably floating around on the Internet somewhere as well.

The back-and-forth of the employment process has been made nearly instantaneous by the 'net. Apply for a modeling job on a leather site with a custom digital photo snapped moments before, and do it via e-mail or perhaps an interactive form built into the web site. Hear back from the producers hours or even minutes after you contact them. Already snapped the pix? Upload them to the producer's site. Receive your fee via your favorite on-line payment processing company. Aside from actually taking the pictures or video, the whole modeling job could take less than an hour, and be done without ever meeting your employer.

Of course, that's an extreme example. I generally prefer to do my own shoots. Not only do I enjoy meeting the models, I have control over all the technical and artistic aspects. That generally means one of us has to travel (95% of the time it's the model), so the process can take days, weeks or even months to gel.

MODEL

For the purposes of this book, a "model" is anyone appearing in still pictures and/or short video scenes. Adult-content video is often produced on a per-scene basis, and the acting chops required of a participant are very limited – usually one or two emotions, tops. C'mon, crawling all over a custom Corvette in a bikini, pretending to wash it, requires you to express two ideas: "Oooh, this water is cold!" and, "Washing this car makes me horny." Even your community college acting teacher would be hard pressed to call that high drama.

Also, I'm going to admit being sexist throughout this book. The information presented here is 99% accurate for male hopefuls, but you'll find me referring mostly to women here. The main reasons:

1) Most of the content I'm talking about will feature women, because it's produced for heterosexual males – the predominant "cash sources" on the Internet.

2) This is a very shallow business. There are opportunities for almost any woman on the 'net, from the most beautiful to the least physically attractive, because there's a horny guy out there somewhere willing to pony up cash and see any and all forms of feminine pulchritude. Guys, you pretty much need to be physically striking – very handsome or downright ugly – before anyone is willing to give you dime one to appear on camera. Straight, bi and lesbian women know it's about the cash, and it's straight males who will likely be ogling them. Straight guys tend to freak out when you tell them it's gay males who will be paying the big bucks to check them out.

3) Content producers rarely jump niches. They shoot for one group because they understand it. I shoot primarily women. Not because I'm homophobic, either. It's for the same reason I don't shoot rope bondage scenes – I know my knots suck, and that's what bondage aficionados will be looking at, more than the model. So I leave that to the bondage folks, who do it much better than I. And that's why I'm writing a book targeted at female adult-content models – it's what I can knowledgeably write about.

MY PET PEEVES

These are things that piss me off. While they may not be "against the rules" per se, they really irritate me. If you do any of them, it immediately brands you as a total amateur. People like me will refuse to work with you. There are people who look for rank amateurs because they're ripoff artitists themselves, and want to take advantage of the innocents abroad in the world.

Aside from getting ripped off, you just look like an idiot for doing any or all of the following.

Self Photos

If you aspire to be a professional model, do not send or post a photo of yourself taken from a cell phone at arm's length. No flash-in-the-mirror pix or grainy webcam snaps, either.

First of all, these are generally very poor quality, dark and out of focus. They don't give anyone a good idea of what you look like.

More important, if you're serious – I mean **SERIOUS** – about modeling, you'll share that desire with someone you trust. At the very least, they can help you by taking photos of you. Aside from that, they can be a sounding board, and help you go over the offers you get for shoots.

Yes, there are *consumers* who like the "I shot my own picture" content. Photographers are not looking for people to shoot themselves, though. Just don't do it.

Goofy Names

Back in the day, Prince decided to change his name to an androgynous symbol. But what did you call this musician? His promotional team quickly decreed that the press and public must refer to him as "The artist formerly known as Prince." That worked for a while, since he was already famous. But when his fame failed? He changed his name back to "Prince."

The Internet is a powerful tool, available to both genius and fool. Please, don't be a fool. When you name yourself something like "MiZb00tyl1c10Us" or "xOXokiMMeeLuvxOXo" you're telling potential employers you lack maturity. How am I supposed to address you on the phone if your modeling name is "6!*#9" ? And don't call yourself "triXXXie" or anything with a lot of X's in it if you're not looking for a hard-core porn job.

I highly doubt your parents gave you your modeling name, which means you've picked it out for yourself. Be aware that any goofy combination of mis-matched letters and numbers as a "name" automatically makes you look stupid. Which means you are saying, "I am stupid." And although modeling is a shallow industry, why would I want to spend time with someone who doesn't value themselves?

Unearned Arrogance

I had a woman call me up and tell me that she would be in town the following week, that her rate was $250/hr with a 3 hour minimum, and that I was going to shoot her. My reply was, "No, I'm not." She then went into a tirade against me, my business, and my other models. I hung up on her. For her sake, I hope she was on drugs, or had some other problem that could be cured.

I actually appreciate arrogance on the part of experts I hire to solve my problems. I want a surgeon who knows what he's doing to be cutting into me, if I need it. An accountant who delivers on a promise to cut my taxes in half can pee in my sink if he wants. But unearned arrogance is not a good thing.

I don't care how good or unique your looks are, or how high your rate is. If you're going to be arrogant, you need to be able promise me something exceptional, and deliver on it. She made no promises, and offered me nothing of value. True, sometimes you can get people to do what you want with a confident attitude, but confidence is not the same as arrogance.

"But wait," you say. "Your tone throughout this whole book is arrogant, Perfetti. And that name – Tony Perfect? What gives you the right to lecture me on unearned arrogance?"

First, I promised you that if you read this book and followed all my advice, you could earn a substantial income from an industry where you can be nearly as lazy as you want. It's happened for others, it can happen for you.

Second, the moniker is alliterative – that is, it's based on how my full name sounds. I am far from perfect, so you might even say "Tony Perfect" is a joke. But at least it's spelled correctly, and I don't use any numbers or symbols.

Poor English

Learn to speak and write proper English. I constantly get e-mails with poor spelling, no punctuation or paragraph breaks, and horrible grammar.

Let me ask you a question: If I'd written this book with information presented in the following manner, could you understand it? Would you have bought the book? Would you do anything I advise? If your answer is anything but "No!" then I'm worried for you – really.

> Im gunna tell u abt what its lik to be a modell it's pretty c00l akshully first you get your picture took and then u make money see what I said aint that kul? u get like all famous an stuf just for like standing arownd in yor undies.

Good communication is essential. There are rules, and you need to know them. Spelling, grammar, punctuation when writing. Enunciation – speaking clearly – when making an oral presentation. Controlling your body language both on and off camera.

Hygiene

Keep yourself clean! You may be hired to model snowsuits, but that doesn't mean you can show up with greasy hair and body funk. If you don't care about you, then why should I?

Keep your nails trimmed and, if they've got polish on them, touch up any imperfections. I may not be specifically shooting your hands, but they'll probably make their way into a shot or scene. If they look bad, they will detract from what we're trying to feature.

Brush your teeth, and carry mints with you just in case.

Wear clean clothes. If you step out of a shower and back into the same dirty clothes you had on, you're going to stink again in less than two minutes, guaranteed.

Carry feminine hygiene products at all times. I don't care if it's not nearly "that time of the month," accidents can and do happen.

Wear deodorant or antiperspirant. If we're shooting an exercise vid where your pits are wet after a workout, I want the liquid to come out of a spray bottle, not your pores. That way I can control the size and shape of the stain, and neither of us has to worry about body funk.

In general, just stay clean, okay?

THE SAIM 9 RULES

If you get nothing else out of this book, tear out this chapter and tape it to your mirror. This is the chapter where you get the best, most basic tips. These are the SAIM 9 Rules, and following them will rocket you down the road to modeling success.

1   SHOW UP, AND BE ON TIME. Modeling, even on a purely porn level, is a job. Treat it that way. As with any other job, you only get paid when you show up. You will beat out other models who are better looking and have more talent and experience if you simply show up. Show up on time for a couple shoots, and you've already earned three-quarters of your reputation as a professional.

2   BE CLEAN. Practice good hygiene on an ongoing basis. Take a shower, brush your teeth, and wash your hair. You need to make sure you don't have pimples or dirt in "those places," so use a mirror to check yourself out, or ask a spouse or trusted friend to look. Some minor blemishes can be covered up, but it's better to minimize the need.

3   BE OVER-PREPARED. Bring several outfits of your own, from casual to classy. Bring make-up and hair supplies. Sure, the producer said there would be a make-up artist on the set. They promised you a wide range of clothing was being sent in for the day. But go back to Rule #1 – the make-up artist may not follow it. The wardrobe people could have had an emergency. Save the day by being over-prepared, and you'll be very much in demand.

4   TREAT IT AS A BUSINESS. Be prepared to demonstrate that you can talk intelligently about what you do. Find out as much as you can about your chosen content niches. Have copies of your ID ready, and actually read the model release and/or contract before you sign them. If you can get a copy of them in advance of the shoot, that's even better.

Learn how to negotiate your rate, and know what a good rate is for the content and geographical location.

If you've set limits on content ("I'll do up to and including topless"), stick with them. Do what you agreed to do, but don't be tempted to go further without stopping and renegotiating.

Money is only a tool. It cannot buy happiness, no matter what someone tells you in the middle of a shoot. Set aside some of your earnings for expenses, some for fun and some for food and lodging. Don't show up for a shoot flat-ass broke. If things have changed and you find you can't work and get paid, you'll need to get back home some how.

5   TREAT IT AS A CRAFT. Take modeling and/or acting lessons. Learn how to move, how to show emotion and feeling not only with your face, but by body language as well. Take lessons in hair and make-up, in photography, videography and lighting. If you learn what the people around you on a shoot are trying to accomplish, you have a better chance of learning and growing at your own chosen job. If the producer gets stuck for a grip or other help on a job, you may have a second job.

6   BE FLEXIBLE. Be willing to travel a little outside your normal range for a shoot. Be willing to accept alternate forms of payment – copies of your photos and videos, theater tickets, restaurant gift certificates, and such – in partial payment. (Negotiate this first, of course.) Be ready to do a different kind of shoot, depending on the availability of other models, clothing, props or locations.

7   BE UNDERSTANDING. You're working with other human beings, and they have good days and bad days, just like you. A producer's pet may die, another model's car may fail to start, or a house the producer plans on using may get flooded. Things out of their control happen to people all the time. When they do, cut them some slack. Remember: at least the tragedy didn't happen to you. And when it does, you'll appreciate the same type of understanding.

8   DON'T DO DRUGS. This is not a moral directive. I'm all for personal choice. What I'm saying is, illicit and illegal drugs will mess with your perception and your body. Drugs change your personality – make you flakey and unreliable. They mess with your values. They can also change your body, change your skin tone, your hair, your nails. You spend all of your cash on the drugs, and not on healthy food. Eventually, producers will no longer want to deal with you, either because your attitude stinks, you look like crap, or more likely – both.

Drugs or modeling, your choice. You can't do both for very long.

9 BE PRO-ACTIVE. Don't sit on your butt waiting to be discovered. Find jobs on your own – small shoots lead to larger shoots.

If you follow the SAIM 9 Rules™, you will be working as a successful adult Internet model in no time.

MAKIN' IT LEGAL

DISCLAIMER: In no way is this chapter purporting to give legal advice. Neither the author nor the editor are lawyers. We don't even play them on TV. Laws change, and are always subject to interpretation by the courts. The only firm advice we give is 1) Educate yourself by taking a business law/contracts course at your local institute of higher learning, and 2) Retaining a lawyer is a good investment.

Before I shoot any model, I take copies of two of her ID's. Then, I sit her down and go over my model release and contract. I try to get her to read and understand the release long before we get to the time of the actual shoot. My release and contract are available for download in PDF format from my modeling site. I've never had a potential model refuse to sign, but with many of them I've seen their eyes glaze over as I explain it. That's bad for them. I could be screwing them over – many of them actually expect that – and they wouldn't know.

I wrote my contract with a minimum of legalese. Almost all of it is in plain, direct English. I've intentionally made it easy to understand.

Any potential model, mine or any other producer's, really needs to read and understand what they're being asked to sign before they sign it. Not all releases are written in plain English, and not all producers, sadly, are concerned with the rights or benefits of their models.

A contract is a legally binding agreement spelling out the terms of an exchange, containing an offer and and acceptance. An oral (spoken) contract is just as binding as a written one, it's just slightly harder to enforce.

For instance, "I'll give you $100 if you take your clothes off and let me take pictures," is an offer. "Okay" is a legal acceptance. If this conversation sounds familiar, you've made an oral contract. The fact that there is an agreement for of exchange – money for pictures – is pretty obvious. But the problem is that the terms are not very clear. How far must the model strip down? Just to her shoes? Down to her birthday suit? When does she get paid – before or after?

Sample Contracts

On the SAIM web site, there are links to several example model releases and contracts.

Please visit our site and take a look at them.

www.AdultModeling
Book.com/ml

19

And what will appear in the pictures? It's only implied that the model will pose. I could mean, "Stand beside me, naked, while I take pictures of the sofa."

You need to make sure the terms of the offer are spelled out clearly. If you want them to be even clearer, nothing says you can't ask for a plain English clause to be added. Once the explanation is added, you're both free to re-evaluate the contract before signing. Unless both parties agree, it's still a no-go.

A big part of any model contract is the concept of "rights." This basically is what you are exchanging for the money you receive. Who owns the content you'll be helping produce, and how may the images, videos, etc. be used? Will the model be allowed to use (that is, have the rights to) any of the content, and what are the conditions for her use of it?

My contract states that my company owns any and all content produced. The model is allowed to use digital copies of content that I provide her, as long as she doesn't remove any copyright notices or other marks of ownership I put on or in the images.

I'm not trying to be a jerk. Actually this arrangement is meant to help both of us. She gets to use some great promotional pieces, and having my info on them not only promotes me but protects both of us in case someone else tries to use the picture (or video clip) without permission or payment.

A contract is only valid if the goods or services being exchanged are legal. For instance, you can't have a legal contract offering to pay a pound of crystal meth to the person who murders your neighbor. You may have an offer, an acceptance and a (very literal) execution, making the contract technically flawless, but it's not legal.

Why am I bringing this up? Because you need to be as sure as possible that what you're being asked to do on camera is legal.

Don't agree to rob a store on tape. Don't snort, shoot, pop or smoke illegal drugs in front of a camera. Many sexual and non-sexual activities are often simulated for mainstream TV shows and movies. But don't let the producer talk you into actually doing them on-camera "to add realism" or some such bullshit. Having a contract to break the law for pay just adds more years to your sentence. "I only smoked crack before robbing the liquor store because I signed a contract, your honor," does not move the responsibility to the producer.

Be careful when agreeing to produce some fetish and hard-core sexual content as well. Depending on where you are producing it, and how the contract is written, any form of sexual interaction for pay may be considered prostitution. Even blowing smoke in someone's face can be prosecuted as a form of assault!

Again, we are not lawyers, but before participating in this type of content, talk to someone who specializes in these types of legal issues. Remember, something perfectly legal in one state could get you a stiff penalty in another.

Which brings me, at last, to kiddie porn. Just don't do it. If you are approached by a producer to star in or help recruit for kiddie porn, report them to the authorities immediately. These soulless scumbags are a sickness and a danger to everyone around them. They bring down the entire industry, not to mention all of society. Killing them is too quick and merciful. If I had my way, I'd tattoo "PEDOPHILE" on their foreheads and stick them in the meanest, nastiest Federal penitentiary I could find, filled with murderers, rapists, arsonists and other fine folk. The prison population would make sure these people had a good taste of hell here on earth before sending them along the real thing in the afterlife.

But that's strictly my opinion. I digress. . .

You need to be aware of what you're doing, and where you're doing it. For example, taking an eighty year old grandmother, putting her in a school uniform and pigtails, and having her say "I'm only sixteen, but I love sex" could, in some states, be interpreted as child pornography. So be careful about what kind of content in which you agree to appear.

WHAT'S IN A NAME?

There are two basic ways a new adult content model has of differentiating herself. The first is her look, which can be changed and manipulated. The second is her modeling name, which should not be changed if she wants to keep getting business.

There are several industries where using your own name with the public is either a bad idea, or simply not done. Actors and actresses are actually required by their unions to have a unique name, so that there's no confusion in the public's mind, and no confusion on the part of producers writing them checks. Radio and TV on-air personalities often use variations of their real names, either to make pronunciation easier or to remove any trace of ethnicity. Even waitresses sometimes feel compelled to give false names to their customers in case one of them decides she's worth stalking.

The most obvious fake names are used by strippers and porn stars. Some times they're created by the (usually male) producers and club owners, but nowadays are often "made up" by the woman. I qualify that because of a very important problem – they pick a name they've heard elsewhere. Problems happen when the two names collide in the public eye. At that point, someone's not happy.

Violet Blue. A name used by two different women in the sex industry. One is an author, and one is an ex porn star. It came to a head when the author wanted the web site owned by the porn star. Author sued porn star, charging her with trademark violation, dilution, and unfair business practices. Because of a lack of funds to fight the law suit, the actress has changed her porn name to Noname Jane, and been forced to turn over the rights to the branded URL (VioletBlue.net) she was using to make money. She, and the video companies that own the movies she starred in, will face an uphill battle if they try to promote her old material. The companies would have to remove her old name from all the materials, including packaging, advertisements, and film credits. It's just not worth it for them.

Not that this will happen to you, but you should be careful about the name you choose to work under. A name should be easy to remember, yet identifiable. If you decide to get into edgy content, like bondage or some other fetish, a name that alludes to your chosen field may help every-one – the producer will remember you, and the name will be "promotable" to the target audience. (Inane names like "Giggles LaMour" are one of the main pieces of ammunition for the folks who believe adult material objecti-fies women – the viewers can't possibly see the performer as a person with a brain.)

On an interesting side note, try picking up your local phone book and look in the yellow pages under "hair dressers" or "salons." This is the oth-er major industry where people seem to put a great deal of time and cre-ativity into coming up with the most ridiculous names possible. Hair Port? Weave The People? Oh, please!

Today, you have essentially two options in coming up with a modeling name. First, you could come up with a totally innocuous, generic name (Melody Henderson, Shawna Anthony, etc.). Or you could make one up. In either case – even if you decide to use your own real name – jump on the Internet and plug the name into one or more search engines. If anyone else is using that name for modeling, pick another one. If you're going to be doing extreme content, make sure no-one else with that name is likely to be offended and sue you. If you're committed to adult modeling, you might consider trademarking the name, and protecting it yourself.

Whatever you do, I urge you not to use a name made out of symbols, numbers and alternating case letters. If a producer can't pronounce your name, he won't call you. Even worse than using a silly conglomeration of letters and numbers is answering the phone and saying, "Oh, you can just call me Jill." If you want to be called Jill, then call yourself Jill. Real pro-ducers want to know they'll be working with mature individuals who won't cry if asked to take off their blouse, or won't spread silly rumors about them. The name you choose for yourself will help them determine if you're mature enough to handle the business.

Unique spellings using real letters are a good choice, but don't overdo it. "Tina" might be creatively spelled "Teena" "Teenah" or even at a stretch "Tea'Na." But again, go too wild, and people won't know how to pronounce it.

Your modeling name is one of the top ways you'll market yourself. Pick a good one, and promote it wisely.

MANAGERS - GOOD AND BAD

I fully admit to being prejudiced. I haven't had many good experiences with managers and agents. When I'm approached by one who really does their job well (and it is a job, boys and girls), my jaw drops to my chin.

Too many "managers" or "agents" are simply boyfriends whose sole skill seems to be stealing money out of the model's hands. They have sex with the model, handle all the money, and refuse to account for their time or expenses.

I've seen a number of photographers who call themselves mangers as well. They're better than boyfriends at the job, but don't really seem to be able to give you the time and attention a real, dedicated manager does. They screen e-mails, and can generally tell other real photographers from "perverts with cameras," but that's about it.

Now, before I'm lynched by an angry mob, let me say clearly and for the record: professional managers and agents can do wonders for your career, and provide valuable services for their pay. I just don't see many of these folks; that's all I'm saying.

Managers and agents do two different jobs. Brief job descriptions might be:

Agent

This person lines up work for the model, and helps publicize them. They contact producers, set modeling appointments, and make sure the model's name and image get in front of "the right people."

Manager

Day-to-day tasks are left to the manager. They get the model up in the morning, make sure she's packed, get her to the shoot, and get her back home and in bed, ready to start again the next day. They make sure the model has copies of all the paperwork she's signed, they make trips to pick up cof-

---

Represent

You'll be working hard to present yourself in the best light possible. You want to make sure your manager or agent is well-dressed, well-spoken, and presents themselves professionally.

Don't let them ruin all your hard work!

fee and sanitary napkins, they tell jokes to disgruntled producers and gently insert themselves between the model and her lunatic fans.

As a beginning model, you need at least a working knowledge of both jobs. If you decide you're not going to do them, you need to be very careful about selecting people to fill these roles. Being your best friend, your lover, or a concerned relative does not qualify someone as a good agent or manager. They need business skills, experience, and a fair amount of street savvy. They need both tenacity and tact.

TYPES OF PRODUCERS

When you're looking for new producers to work with, you need to know a little more than what type of content they shoot. Ideally, you want to know where they are in their career as a photographer or videographer.

We'll take a look at some of these levels. Be aware – we're painting with a big brush, here. We're making generalizations. Please remember that each producers is a complex individual, and not just a "type" listed in a book.

GWC

At the very bottom of the heap (in more ways than one) is the GWC, or Guy With Camera. You used to be able to tell these guys immediately – they had disposable film cameras, met you at motels with hourly rates, and had no paperwork for you to sign. Some of them truly believe their actions are harmless. They aren't.

Now, with professional quality digital cameras under $1,000, and personal digitals under $100 giving pictures suitable for the web, it's a little harder to tell who these guys are.

Generally, though, these people are after as much sexual contact as they can get, for as little money as possible. Their joy in life is to screw you, and then screw you over.

Don't go anywhere near these guys. If you find one, you should warn all other models and producers you know.

Rank Amateur

These folks may look like GWC's, if you're one of the first people to shoot with them, except that they tend to have better equipment and pay better. They also have a plan (hare-brained maybe) for making money with the content they're shooting.

If you want to take an RA under your wing, that might keep them from becoming a GWC. Remember, money and referrals come from professionalism.

An RA has probably read a few books, but is fairly nervous about telling you what to do, or discussing content. They probably will ask you for ID, and even have paperwork for you to sign. Make sure you ask for – and receive – copies of the contract before leaving.

RA's have a vague idea of what they're going to do with the content they shoot. Feel free to help them as much as you can. The more they make the more (and more often) they'll be inclined to pay you.

Serious Amateur

SA's have a lot of expensive equipment, and may even have turned a spare room or basement into a studio. They're careful to give you copies of your contract, and may even offer you copies of some of what you shoot with them. SA's are more comfortable than RA's talking about explicit content, but may still offer to leave while you disrobe.

They are probably supplementing their income with the results of your shoot, and whatever money they make probably goes back into equipment and model fees.

Semi-Pro

In between the SA and Beginning Professional. Unless you ask them about their day job, you might not know the difference.

Beginning Professional

Works out of a real studio, has no other day job, although he may shoot weddings on the side, claiming "it's not what I do for a living." He's probably the only one in the studio, but if he was smart (and feel free to suggest this) he'd get a model in there to help him wrangle equipment, and pay her back by shooting her for free.

28

BP's have props and some costumes, and everything is probably clean, although disorganized from lack of assistance.

You can learn a lot from BP's if you offer to trade your assistance in exchange for a better quality portfolio.

Established Professional

Busy! Lots of helpers. You'll probably get coiffed by one person, made up by another, costumed, lit and posed by even more assistants. Some times an assistant will shoot sample photos first and show them to the EP.

Finally the EP will step in, make a few tweaks, and press the button.

Keep your eyes and ears open, and your mouth shut, when working with an EP. You can learn more from them in one day than you do from SA's in a year.

Attitude Types

Creepy

"C'mere, baby. Let me adjust your bra for you. Oh, you're not wearing one? Even better. Let me show you my rat farm, it's down in my basement. Where ya goin' baby? I thought we had something!"

You get enough of these guys in stores and on subways. Don't encourage them by shooting with them.

Arrogant

Any level. True arrogance is a justifiable confidence in your own ability. Being arrogant and being a jerk don't have to go hand-in-hand, but that concept is beyond some people.

Timid

Usually RA's and BP's, who are less likely to be sure of themselves. "What do you want to do?" You end up being the art director.

"Artiste"

SA's and above – can be distant, but sometimes produce jaw-dropping work.

Strong, Silent Type

Few words, quietly spoken. Seem sure of what they're doing.

Mr Chaos

Loud environment, changes mind frequently, can't find anything. May literally shoot from the hip.

Laid Back

Everything's cool. Will often ask for your input, even show you raw content.

Busy Professional

Barely civil, but not because he's a bad guy. Too busy to talk.

Jerk

Yells at everyone. Not happy unless everyone else is unhappy. Rude on purpose.

POINTS OF REFERENCE

Making a business connection with someone on-line is very easy to do. Actually, I'd say it's *way too easy* to do. It's easier and cheaper to fake a professional web site than it is to buy entry-level photographic equipment, even with the constant drop in photo equipment prices.

But remember, this uncertainty goes both ways. A potential employer is also taking a chance that you're accurately stating your experience and qualifications.

What's either of you to do?

In building a portfolio (either photographer or model), one of the most important sections is the reference or testimonial section. This is where you list the people you've worked with who will say good things about you, and who can verify the tings you've said about yourself. You should have some way prospective employers can check with these people. The best thing is to have your references write a positive comment you can quote in your portfolios. These testimonials can make a big difference in the number and quality of jobs you're offered.

On both sides of the "job fence" though, these references need to be checkable to be of any value

Checking References

Let's say you've searched a portfolio site for producers who shoot the kind of content you'd like to do. You sort through the twenty or so portfolios your search turned up, and you pick three that look interesting.

There are several things you should do to check out these potential employers. Each of them should list their own web site in their portfolio. You want to get as much information as possible about these producers, in as short a time as possible. The first thing you should do is run a series of web searches. Run searches based on their personal web address, their name, their e-mail address, and their telephone number, if they list it.

In the results of the searches, you're looking for two main things: Are there a lot of negative comments associated with them? Second, where and how often are they mentioned professionally? Obviously the perfect producer will have a combination of minimum negativity and maximum credentials, but there's probably going to be a different combination.

Back to our example, two of the producers list several models each in their profiles as references. You should contact them, probably via e-mail or with the site's internal messaging system, and introduce yourself. Then, ask them for their experiences with that particular producer. How much work have they done together? Was this producer safe, sane, reliable and professional? Would they, in short, recommend that producer as someone to work with?

Example

> *Hi, this is Gwen Kix, bikini model. You were listed as a reference in Joe Doaks' profile. I'm considering contacting him for some work.*
>
> *I'd appreciate it if you'd take a minute and tell me about your experience with Joe. Was he professional? Did he keep his promises? Where did you shoot, and what kind of content did you produce? Were his pay rates higher, lower or in-line with industry averages?*
>
> *Anything you could tell me – positive or negative – would be sincerely appreciated, and will be kept in strictest confidence.*
>
> *Thank you for your time. I hope to hear from you soon.*
>
> *Sincerely,*
>
> *Gwen Kix*

Weeding through the replies you get can be a little tough. Always expect some kind of mild negative feedback. Occasionally, you'll get a nasty letter, ripping the producer apart. Since we're all human, this is to be expected. But as long as you don't get a bunch of negative replies, you'll probably be okay contacting the producer for a job.

It's often a good idea to let the producer know you've checked his "refs" and ask him about any negative feedback up front.

What do you do with that third producer who doesn't have refs in his profile? He might be brand new, or he might simply not understand the power and importance of references. So you'll have to ask him for some.

Tell the producer you found his profile and would like to discuss the possibility of working together. You notice he doesn't have any references listed – could he supply you with contact info for some of his models who have done the kind of content you want to do?

There are some people who have an attitude of superiority. "Why should I bother to give you references? I'm the best at what I do! If you need to check me out, I don't want to work with you." Please, don't be one of these people. Professionals appreciate the fact that you care enough about your own career and safety to ask for – and check – references. While the obnoxious people may be famous in their own small niche, or their own small mind, they're usually as well known for being jerks as they are for their prowess in front of or behind the camera.

Giving References

At some point, you'll probably be asked to serve as a reference for a producer, or for other talent and technicians (make up artists, lighting techs, etc.) with whom you've worked. Relax, take a deep breath! It's not as scary as it seems.

There are six things you want to keep in mind about responding to someone's request for a reference. If you keep them in mind when you're writing your reply, everything should go smoothly.

Be honest

Don't try to tell the person what you think they want to hear. Just tell them what happened.

Be specific

"Last year some time" is not a good time reference, but "September 19th" is. "We shot some stuff" isn't helpful, but "We shot bikini and topless content" is. Without overwhelming the person in minute details, be as specific as possible.

Be brief

The person requesting the reference wants a note back, not a novel. Be as brief as you can, while still keeping to the specifics. If something unusual, either positive or negative, happened, it might warrant a longer answer. But again, be brief.

State facts, not emotion

"He tried to kill me!" is not the same as, "He approached me with a knife, without telling me it was rubber. I got scared, then mad when I figured out it was a fake." The second has emotion in it, but explains the facts of the situation much better than the first.

Answer direct questions

Again, you don't want to give someone an answer you think they want to hear. However, don't be afraid to answer a direct question with an honest, direct answer. "Did you feel safe with him?" "Yes, I felt safe at all times."

State your recommendation

End the information part of the note with a final, specific recommendation. If it needs to be qualified, that's okay. "You asked about shooting adult nude content with Joe, Since I didn't do that, I can't say what your experience will be like, or what he'd pay you, but I would certainly recommend him as someone to shoot bikini and topless content with."

Remember, when a recommendation you've written is quoted in someone else's portfolio, or on their web site, it could lead to a job for you. It shows you know the industry, and are a professional.

LET'S DO BUSINESS

If you don't treat modeling as a business, you're essentially treating it as a hobby, like stamp collecting or growing petunias. Businesses make money. Hobbies cost you money. Which one of these was the reason you thought about becoming an adult Internet model?

I thought so.

Types Of Businesses

Do I have to remind you again we are not lawyers? This is general information only.

A business is a legal entity under which someone sells goods and services. That is to say, starting a business is like giving birth to a child. Most businesses stand apart from their owners and employees for one or more reasons.

The simplest business is the DBA, or "Doing Business As" certificate. Let's say you decided to start a rug cleaning business. You wanted to call it "Julie's Rug Cleaning." In most states, you'll visit the county office and fork over a small fee. You'll be required to check their records to make sure no-one else is doing business under that name. If it's all clear, they issue you a certificate. You can now advertise under the name, and you'll take the DBA to your bank so they know you'll be accepting checks under that name. A DBA doesn't really provide any legal protection (we'll be getting to that shortly).

If you decide to start a business with someone else, the simplest form of business is the Partnership. There are several different types of partnerships, including General, Limited and Professional, but the basic premise is the same as with the DBA. Instead of "I am calling myself. . ." you're saying "We're calling ourselves. . ."

A Corporation is the kind of business the major players create. Corporations are meant to exist apart from the people who create them, and are meant to outlive individuals. They have boards of directors, officers and employees. Corporations can be either private - wholly owned by one or more individuals as a private enterprise - or public, where anyone may buy shares (little pieces of the company) and share in the company's profits. There are also several types of corporations, some intended strictly for small businesses. Since a corporation is a unique entity, it provides some legal protection for it's directors and employees. The business itself can "step between" legal trouble and the people who work for it, in some cases. Corporations can cost a lot to set up, and running them is a complex process – a business in it's own, actually.

A hybrid that has been gaining popularity during the last decade is the Limited Liability Company, or LLC. It provides some of the legal and financial protection of a true corporation, but is meant to be small and flexible. LLCs have "members" as opposed to owners and employees.

I'm partial to LLCs myself, but you should consult a lawyer to help you decide which kind of business is the best for your particular needs. Speaking of them...

Lawyers

You need one. Regardless of all the lawyer jokes you've heard and told, they can play an important part in keeping you and yours legally safe.

I would suggest you find a lawyer who has experience in the adult entertainment industry. Yes, it might be embarrassing to call up a law office and say, "Do you work with people who take their clothes off for a living?" Your state should have a legal association that helps people find the right kind of representation. Check the Internet or even you local library.

A good lawyer will help you interpret modeling contracts, and help you decide what kind of business entity you should create. There are cheaper, do-it-yourself books and kits on the Internet, but they don't come with specific legal advice. Consider carefully if you'll want to forgo legal advice.

A lawyer can also help determine the legality of certain types of content. If you're working only in one state, that should be simple. But if you're being paid in multiple states, he should be able to either check your legal status in that state, or find you another lawyer there who can.

Accountant

Declare your income, and pay your taxes. I do not advocate trying to hide money from the government. That said, a good accountant can help you legally pay the least amount of taxes. Doing it yourself is okay, but then you're not in the accounting business, you're in the modeling business. So who would do a better job?

Try to be as organized as you can. Keep every receipt and file it away neatly (or at least cram them all in a shoe box). If you drive, keep a detailed mileage and expense log. Depending on your records and the type of business you've set up, you may be able to deduct the cost of clothes and keeping them clean. Love shoes? If you're doing foot modeling, you might be able to write them off as business equipment. But only a good accountant knows for sure.

Keep some cash socked away for taxes. Depending on your business, you'll probably be paying quarterly estimated taxes, and they'll want it when it's due. Hiding from the authorities will only have them estimate the maximum tax and then assess you penalties for not paying. Run from the tax man, and you'll need a good tax attorney to dig you out when they find you. That won't be cheap.

Another benefit of keeping your business above board is that you won't have to deal with ripoff artists. I can't tell you how many young women I've dealt with whose "managers" (boyfriends) have convinced them to register that new car in his name, to keep her safe from The Tax Man. Two weeks later, he's driving off in what is legally his new car with some bimbo, and the model is stuck paying out the nose for nothing.

You'll want a checking account with a bank – something a little more well known than the Last National Bank of Podunk. If you're traveling, you need to be able to deposit cash and checks locally. As your credit grows and improves, you'll want a business-only credit card that you use for emergencies and unexpected expenses. Notice I didn't say, "for going on vacation."

Your accountant will appreciate you (and maybe even lower his fee) if you keep track of all your transactions in an accounting program. Many small business owners use the de facto standard, QuickBooks. Your accountant may have another choice, but try to get something that's simple to use, where you can take five minutes each day and update everything. Then, when he needs it, you'll be able to send him the transaction file, and he (or she) can get to work reducing your tax bill.

Financial Planning

When you've paid off all your bills, you need to set aside some money for the future. Money is a tool, and it can do some heavy lifting for you if you put it to work. At minimum, you'll need some kind of retirement account. Self employed people can set up a Self Employment Pension (SEP). You can also open what's called an IRA (Individual Retirement Account), or some other type of retirement plan.

However, that money is probably just sitting there, waiting for the right combination of factors to come into play before you can get your hands on it. It's probably not going to be doing work for you.

You should consider some other type of investments, something that's more aggressive and likely to yield a substantial return on your investment. Property is the 800 lb gorilla of investments – it can make you a lot of money or it can tear your (financial) arms off.

My advice is to interview a number of financial planners at the same time you're doing research of your own. Don't dump money in the lap of the first person you meet. Ask your lawyer and accountant for their recommendations. Ask the producers you work with who they use, and what kind of investments they have.

As you ask questions and do research, you'll find that only a small percentage of the population has any investments. Even a couple small accounts, to which you make regular deposits, will quickly put you ahead of most of the population. That's the whole point of this book! Anyone can take their clothes off and get paid for it – they'll probably be broke again in an hour. The idea is to become a professional and make a good living from doing it.

Financial planning, like so many of the other topics mentioned in the book, is worth an entire college course in itself. While I can't tell you exactly what to do, I think it's important enough that I point you in the right direction. You really should to set aside a portion of your income and then put it to work via investments.

Computer

Get a good portable computer. Load it only with the software you'll need to do business – email, accounting software, something to edit photos with, a word processor and maybe software that helps you create and maintain your web site. (We're coming to that, too.) One small, simple game, but that's it – this is meant for work, not play.

A good, rugged portable inkjet printer would be a good idea as well, for printing out letters and contracts.

You need a "road warrior" kit when going on the road. At minimum, you'll want a good surge protector – not just an outlet strip, but something that protects everything plugged in from surges and spikes. At home, you'll want a good uninterruptable power supply (UPS for short). You also need to carry duplicate power cords, cables that can connect you to the Internet in places without wi-fi, and cleaning supplies. I would also suggest carrying a small collection of USB flash drives and blank CDs or DVDs for making data backups.

Portfolio

You will want to be on several portfolio web sites, and to be active on a couple. By "active" I mean regularly updating your portfolio, reading and responding to your messages, and reading and posting messages on their forums. Your profile should tell potential employers exactly what you're willing to shoot, who you're willing to work with, and your rules for travel. Link back to producers you've worked with, and ask them to do the same for you. If they've written kind words about you, find a way to quote them in your profile.

You should also have a print portfolio with you at all times. It should contain the very best of your work, along with tear sheets – copies of ads or whatever that have been taken out of various publications. A "hard" portfolio should also contain the best testimonial letters you've received from producers, models and other industry personnel with whom you've worked.

For both print and on-line portfolios, you'll want to try to include samples of all the kinds of content you're willing to pose for. If you promote yourself as a bikini model, include the best ones. If you're doing fetish, include shots of those areas. You get the idea.

Keep your portfolios updated as much as possible! If you change your hair length or color, and don't have a new picture, mention it in the profile and in all your e-mails with producers. Make sure you mention all scars, piercings and body modifications, no matter how small. You don't want to lose a job you've traveled to because of something you forgot to mention.

Professionalism

Yes, I keep going back to this point over and over again. You might think it was actually important for some reason!

Would you expect an "expert auto mechanic" to be working out of an abandoned dry cleaning shop, dressed in his ClownBurger uniform? What about showing up for an appointment at your accountant's office and he's not there? Or having your surgeon stumble into the operating room wearing shorts and smoking a cigar? None of these things is acceptable. None of these are examples of professionalism.

You want to be known as someone who knows what they're doing, shows up on time, and keeps their promises. If there's a problem, you tell the people you're supposed to work with as soon as possible. You're prepared for the unexpected. You are, in short, professional.

A very important tool in business. Not enough people in any industry possess this trait. If you are professional, you'll get more jobs, and command higher rates.

Rates

Well, I know where to start. After that, things get a little confusing.

The lowest rate is where you actually pay the photographer for shooting you. Ideally, you want to limit this type of shoot. As a model, you pay someone else cash only if you can't find another way to get the shots done. You might want work done by one particular producer, or you want to shoot a particular type of content that's expensive to set up, or you want to own the content completely, and not have any copies appear anywhere else.

The next lowest rate is actually a trade. It used to be called TFP, or Time in exchange For Prints. You donate your time, and the photographer gives you copies of the work. With everything going digital, you'll probably be offered TFCD (Time For CD) or TFDVD. Great for building portfolios, or for working with promising producers who are currently too poor to pay you. You want people to nurture your career, so you might consider doing the same. It may be a model who's trying her hand behind the camera, or a student who's only building his portfolio. Even lawyers work for free sometimes. I ask that you consider the situation and the person before you say "No."

As a beginning model, with little or no experience, you're not going to be offered the top rates. The more positive testimonials you get from producers, the better reputation you'll get in the industry. The better your reputation, the more you'll be able to charge.

In some aspects of adult modeling, the no-show rate can be as high as 80%. That means producers are stiffed by eight out of 10 women who promise to show up and work. If you become known as someone who shows up when you say you will (see Professionalism above) you can demand just about anything you want – higher rates, specific make-up, a bowl of green candy. . . almost anything.

You'll want to review offers posted on web sites, and talk to models and producers about what the going rates are in any particular place for the type of content you're looking to model for. In some areas, the rates for hard core adult content are actually less than they are for, say, clothed bondage. One hard core model I knew got ticked because she was actually in more demand as a foot & shoe model than as a porn star. She loved having sex on camera, but producers made more money off her legs and feet. Go figure!

The final thing I can say about rates is: if it seems too good to be true, it probably is. If someone is offering you $200/hr to model parkas, either they've got something dastardly in mind, or you'll be in the Arctic freezing your toes off because no other model in her right mind is willing to do the shoot. Do not be tempted into doing content you wouldn't otherwise do just for the money. It won't be worth it in the long run.

Negotiation

Bargaining. Haggling. Kids do it all the time. "I'll be your best friend if you give me a cookie. Let me stay up until eight and I'll go right to sleep, I promise!" Almost every part of your life as a model will involve negotiation.

Volumes have been written on negotiation, but it boils down to dealing with someone and working out an agreement. Let's take rates, as an example. It's only natural that you'll want the highest rate possible, and it's only natural that the producer wants to pay as little as possible for his content. He's trying to maximize his profits, while you're trying to maximize yours. Most times you can come to an agreement. Sometimes you'll "agree to disagree."

One thing to keep in mind: "cost" is not the same as "price." Price is the money you pull out of your pocket to pay for something, while cost is what you give up in addition to – or instead of – something else. For instance, if you fly to a city to work, you pay a price for your ticket. If you do it for a single shoot, that shoot cost you however much time you spent on the plane, a missed trip to Grandma's for dinner, and the hours you'll never get back when you got lost going to the shoot. However, if you book several shoots during that visit, the cost is amortized (spread) across all the shoots, and may make missing Grandma's roast chicken worth your while.

You'll negotiate to minimize your cost, and maximize your price, for the most part. You'll negotiate over content, clothes or the lack of them, and the dates of shoots. Many times you'll negotiate with others, and sometimes you'll negotiate with yourself.

My best advice is to not negotiate your hard and fast rules. I, for example, will never set foot in Connecticut again, for personal reasons, so you can't offer me enough money to get me there. You may do topless, but no actual or implied violence. Whatever your iron clad rules are, don't negotiate them. However, be flexible on other things, like rates, times, and locations. If you really want to do this for a living, it will be a constant give and take with producers, other models, car salesmen and people in general who want a piece of your life.

You can read books and take classes on negotiation. I'd recommend you do so. Getting what you want in life makes for happier, easier living.

Education

Whenever you have the chance to learn something, DO IT. It really doesn't matter what you learn, although as an adult Internet model I'd give my attention first to anything that helps you along in the industry. Classes on modeling, acting, photography, make-up, running a small business. . . all of them will help you immediately. It wouldn't hurt to mention to prospective producers what you've studied that's relevant to a shoot, but I wouldn't list all your completed courses in your profile.

If you can't take courses in one location, consider taking on-line courses, or home study courses. Read books on modeling, the industry, or anything else in which you're interested. Take notes. Participate in peer discussion groups on-line or in person. Do anything you can to keep learning, to keep making yourself more and more valuable − not only to producers, but to the people in your life.

The best education is doing your chosen job and keeping your eyes and ears open. If you find someone you admire, or who obviously has more experience at something than you do, see if they'd be willing to talk with you and teach you what they know. They may not always be open to doing so, or may not have the time. That's all right. Jot down what you've seen and heard anyway, and turn the information over in your mind like the rich mental soil that it is.

I tell all the models I work with, "Every word that drops from my lips is a pearl of wisdom. Every bit of advice I give is perfect, and the way I do things is the only way to do them." Then, I encourage them to try to discredit everything I've told them when they leave. By taking your own time to get better quality knowledge, and to find superior ways of doing a thing, you learn what works in general, and what works for you specifically. Self-education really is the only education. There are thousands of people sitting in college lecture halls who are only wasting time and money because they aren't trying to absorb and sift through all the knowledge coming their way.

Promotion

For people who have trouble talking about themselves, this is the hardest part. But it's actually the heart of this and every other business. Marketing your product – you – is how you wind up with jobs. We've already talked about portfolios, but there are several ways you can help producers find you.

Other chapters will include specific information on aspects of marketing yourself. There are two important ideas I want to get across here:

> ❖Be pro-active
> ❖Promote the benefits of hiring you

> ### Getting Work
>
> Most portfolio sites allow you to search for producers. Do it - don't wait for them .
>
> You should also network with other models in your niche. Ask them who's hiring, and to recommend you.

The most important aspect of marketing is being pro-active. Don't sit on your ass waiting for producers to come crawling out of the woodwork to beg you for a shoot at twice the going rate. It ain't gonna happen. You need to prospect for work, go looking for it high and low. Search the web, visit sites that carry the type of content you want to shoot, and talk with other models and producers. Ask them for leads. Producers and the public are always looking for "the next big thing." But you can't be found unless you stick your head up, wave your hand, and whistle like crazy.

In sales there's an acronym, FAB. It's stand for "Features And Benefits." My advice is forget the Features, sell only the Benefits. The producer doesn't care as much about your looks as he does about the fact that you show up on time, are prepared, and will help promote the content you shot. If he really does care about your looks, that's fine. Sell him on those as secondary points.

I saw a lingerie holiday catalog a few years back. There was a blond in there who had curves in all the right places, but her face was messed up. Her eyes were too close together, her mouth was pinched, and her nose was tiny. Her eyebrows were half way up her very tall forehead. And yet she was featured in the catalog. Why? My guess is that she was hired as a fill-in model, and the main one never showed up. I'd hire her on the spot if I could find her. I already know the biggest benefit of hiring her – she shows up for shoots. Her very nice curves were secondary, and depending on the content, I can live with some imperfections.

Your Own Web Site

You want to have several profiles out on the portfolio web sites. In addition to that, though, it's a good idea to have your own web site as well. The initial benefit is being able to use a "branded" e-mail address (ie Gwen@gwenkixmodel.com). It shows you're professional enough to have your own site, and that you take the business seriously. It automatically gives prospective employers confidence in you.

You'll also be able to control your own content. You can have a mix of examples that run "from mild to wild," as the cliché goes. You can also say anything you want, and it gives you the ability to add other searchable content, like a blog, a bio, and so forth.

You should have a page that lists all the positive feedback you've received from producers you've worked with. Another page should have links (affiliate links, if you've got them – see the Cashing In chapter) to other web sites where your content is shown. You should also have links to each of the different portfolio sites, so that producers can see your profile on the sites where they have memberships.

If you create an e-commerce enabled site, where you can take payment over the 'net for the sale of either physical product or access to digital content, you should consider selling autographed copies of prints via mail.

You may also want to create a paid-members-only area where you sell access to proprietary digital stills, video and or/audio.

You might want to put out a periodic digital or print newsletter for your fans. Do NOT automatically send content, without verifying that the sign-up was from the person whose e-mail address you have. Even a shot of you in a slinky dress sent to a conservative old lady who the neighbor kids signed up for your newsletter "as a joke" could get you shut down.

Unless you want a second career as a web site designer, I'd suggest hiring someone very good to design and host your site. A good site's not going to be cheap. I've seen sites that were designed by the kid next door for $20 and a pizza, and they looked like crap. But it's not so much that you'll want to pay for the initial design. You need to find someone who's going to be around for a while and can make changes to your site when you need them. That's worth more than a small up-front price.

While a complete discussion of web sites, web hosting and e-commerce is beyond the scope of this book, it boils down to: you need a professional quality site if you expect to get professional quality work because of it.

Competition

There's a new face coming into the industry every second. To a certain extent they, along with everyone who came before you, is your competition.

Most people define their competition by terms that are way too narrow. If I am the art director for a swimwear company, and I decide we need a new print ad, I could hire you. Your competition for the job could be everyone who has your measurements, if that's the info I used to decide on a model. It could be everyone with your hair and eye color. It could be everyone in your age range. It could also be no-one: I could decide to hire an illustrator to draw the ad. I could decide to simply show the suit on a hanger.

Your competition could also be all the people who show up for an open casting. That eliminates everyone who looks like you that doesn't show up.

For video work, your competition could be someone with better acting ability or more experience.

Oddly enough, you may be your own competition! I may want a particular look from you that I've seen on-line. Hair a certain way, a certain style of dress, or even a picture of you when you were younger.

The trick with competition is to not have any. You do this by what marketing experts call "positioning."

Take fast food burger joints. They're all the same, really. Burgers, fries, soda and shakes. But each chain has their own way that they want you to think of them. Flame broiled patties. Square patties. The place with the play areas for the kiddies. They want you to mentally lump "the other guys" together while in your mind, they own a "position" of favorability. That way, they have no competition. They want you to think, "I only eat burgers that are fresh, never frozen like at those other places."

If you can create a position in the minds of the producers you work with, they will help you create that position in the minds of other potential employers with their support and testimonials. You'll reinforce that by conforming to, and enhancing, that position.

What you're striving for, and can achieve if you follow the SAIM 9 Rules™, is to be so totally above and beyond the others that *there is no competition for you.*

Business Plan

Normally, this is one of the first things addressed in a business book. Other books are written with the idea that people looking to start a business are already experts in that business. I wanted to make sure you had a good foundation in the adult Internet modeling industry before we got here.

Any plan is just like a road map. "I'm here, I want to get there, and this is how I'm going to do it." That's the basis, and from there it can become very complex, if you're trying to write a plan for becoming a major corporation. Yours doesn't need to be very long, or very complex, at least at first.

A good business plan should be alive, it should change and grow as time goes on. The only way this happens is if you continually have it in front of you, are consulting it, making changes and recording every place you've been and where you want to go next.

The very first thing in making a business plan is setting a goal. It will probably start out very general ("I want to make a lot of money" is the first goal a lot of adult Internet models have) and should very quickly become focused and specific. "In five years, I want a home and family in Wilton Springs. The house will cost about $200k and I'll buy it with the earnings from my modeling career." The first example ("a lot of money") is really a wish. The second is a goal.

Next, you need to know where you are now. Again, a phrase like "I'm broke" is no good. Specifics are best: "I'm 20, unemployed and I live in Podunk Corners. I've had a series of food service jobs, but it's not a career I'm interested in. I like going out to dinner and dressing well, but I don't have the money to do that. I have a high school diploma and want to get a college degree in sociology."

So far, so good. Now, you need to start sketching out the road map you'll follow to get from where you are to where you want to be. If you were driving cross country, the trip would take several days. For that trip, you'd want to break the big trip down into little trips of a day each. Same thing with your business plan. You might break it down something like this.

Getting Started

1. Get friend Suzy to take some sample photos
2. Join 3 portfolio sites from her computer
3. Get first local shoot this week − cash and more sample photos
    A. Buy pay-per-use business phone
4. Update portfolios w/photos & new phone #
5. Look for more producers on portfolio sites
6. Get 2nd paid shoot
    A. Use cash for business cards & 1 new outfit
    B Add minutes to phone

7. Make sure photogs post positive comments on profiles

8. Get 3rd paid shoot - hand out business cards to visiting producers

    A. Use cash to fix car so I can travel farther

    B. Open savings account with $20

This sets up some mini-goals, like 2nd and 3rd jobs, buying a phone, and fixing your car. It's like setting up places you want to visit on Day One of your cross country trip. Once you've taken the first steps, it's important you keep challenging yourself to find new things to do. It's easier to get lazy after a success than after a failure. You'll want to take a couple days off, and the next thing you know you're broke again, and you have to start over at the beginning.

As you go along, keep setting larger and larger personal goals for yourself: a better used car, and then an inexpensive new car. Better roommates, then a small apartment with no roommates. That sort of thing. In between, you'll set and meet career goals the same way: shoot bikini content, then appear on a bikini calendar, then shoot for Vamp swimwear. You'll "draw the dots" for yourself, and then you figure out the actions you need to take to "connect the dots."

It seems like a huge job, I know. The first trick is to break it down into little steps. The second trick is to constantly check and re-check that you're headed for your goal. You may change some of the major steps along the way (from bikini model to foot fetish model, for instance), but don't let the changes stop you. By the way, it's okay to change your goal as you go along. You may find that you have the house and family in four years, but don't want to give up modeling just yet. That's okay, just set a higher goal!

Exit Strategy

You'll want to include this at the end of your business plan, but it's important enough that I'm creating a section just for this topic.

Let's be brutally honest: very few people last as models their whole life. It's possible to do, but their goals change, they develop different priorities, and their looks change. As I've said before, this industry is shallow. That's just the way it is. So you'll want a plan on how to get out, preferably while you're still in demand.

Going back to college is one exit. Starting your own modeling management company or agency might be another. Or becoming a producer yourself. The point is, at some time you'll want to get out from in front of the camera. You'll want to quit doing this for a living. Same thing happens if you're a brain surgeon, by the way. At some point, you want to quit and paint landscapes for a living, or start a little farm. It's natural. The best thing is to plan for it.

You probably got into adult Internet modeling because you needed the cash, or liked the thrill of it. The object now is to squirrel away enough cash that you can, hopefully into your SEP or other retirement account, and your investments. That way you can start a new part of your life without worrying about where your next meal is coming from. If you plan your departure from modeling and set a new series of goals for yourself, the transition will be an easier one.

Whew! This is the longest, and second most important chapter in the book. The most important chapter is the SAIM 9 Rules™, of course. You'll want to read and re-read this chapter as you go along. Hopefully you'll keep this book in your main bag and read it while waiting for the producer to call you to the set (unless you're helping move equipment, or apply make-up, which is even better). You'll get more and more out of the chapter as you gain more and more modeling experience.

AFTER THE SHOOT

The shoot is over. You're back home, or at a hotel on your way to another job. The only thing left for you to do is count your pay, right?

Well, no. Not if you're looking to make this a successful career for yourself, that is.

Ask any business person, and they'll tell you the longest, costliest part of running a business is finding new customers. Most smart business people will want to establish an ongoing relationship with their customers – keep the customers buying from them, rather than searching around.

Establishing that relationship is very easy. Fortunately for you, most models don't bother to even try, which automatically makes you look even better when you follow the following steps.

The first thing you need to do (unless the experience was horrible, and you never want to work with that producer again – it happens) is drop them an e-mail, thanking them for the job. You can follow a formula, but don't forget to personalize the message. Mention people by name, and bring up situations or conversations that happened during the shoot. Close by telling them you want to work with them again. Always try to find positive things to say – people love having their egos stroked.

Does this sound like the Thank You notes your parents made you write? It should. They work, by making the receiver feel appreciated.

Take Notes

Jot short notes about each shoot in your date book.

That way, you can look back and decide who to work with again, and have information in case another model asks about the producer.

SAMPLE

This is where most models fall by the wayside. "I did my job," they say to themselves. "Now all I'm going to do is relax." I'll say it again: as someone who is self-employed, your work doesn't end when the lights get shut off.

Take a moment and think about what happens next on the other side of the camera. Let's say you just posed for a bikini web site. Your pics just show up on the site by magic, and money – which they could use to hire you again – just rolls in out of the blue.

No, I don't think so.

At the very least, someone looks through all the shots and discards every one that's out of focus, or where your head's cut off. Video? Someone needs to edit it. And then the content needs to be prepped for final output.

Buyers don't just show up. There are ads and promos to be placed, the site needs to be talked up on discussion boards, and someone needs to watch the income and expenses.

I'm glossing over it – there's much more to it than that. Frankly, shooting you is the easiest – and probably least costly – part of running the site.

You need to do a lot of the same type of after-shoot work to keep jobs lined up for yourself. Writing a thank-you e-mail to the producer is just the first step.

You need to keep your web presence up-to-date. Upload new pics to your own web site and your on-line portfolios. Post info about your latest shoots to your blog. And you should do it on a regular basis – monthly at least, and more often if you can.

This does a couple things. First, it lets the producers know you appreciate them. Second, it lets your fans (and you do want fans, right?) know where you'll be appearing.

The better portfolio web sites you belong to will also have a discussion board, or forum. Use them to provide reviews, positive and negative, of the producers with whom you work [*NOTE: Some sites don't allow reviews, or separate them into their own area. Read the forum before posting, and know the rules for each board.*] Most people only pass along negative information. "The burgers there are terrible," or "The car salesman screwed me over." If you're known for posting even-handed evaluations, your comments will be more welcome, you'll be seen by everyone in the industry as a professional.

STAY IN TOUCH

You've got to have a way for people to get in touch with you. Several ways are even better. I recommend all of the following, at minimum:

- ❖E-mail
- ❖Wireless phone
- ❖PO Box

Internet:

Some models either can't afford Internet access, or travel around so much that having a home service doesn't make much sense. No matter what, you really need at least one e-mail address. Ideally, you should have a personal address for your family and friends and a business address you give out to producers and put in profiles. Even better, get yourself a web site with your professional name in it, and use branded e-mail to interact with potential employers. Don't like e-mail? Can't use a computer to save your life? Here's a valid reason to hire a manager. Not to beat this particular horse after it's dead, but managers are only worth money if they make you substantially more than what you pay them.

There are literally hundreds of free e-mail services where you can get an address, and check your mail via the web. Many profile sites either offer you that option, or automatically generate an e-mail address for you at their site.

<u>E-mail</u>

1) Don't use AOL or MSN for your business e-mail. They often filter out "adult content" messages and you'll wind up missing out on offers and meeting confirmations. Why use a service that essentially costs you business?

2) Answer all your e-mail. It's especially important to drop those ignorant perverts who ask you for content outside your limits a polite "no thank you." Ignoring a producer, even a small-time one, can lead to a negative image. "She never answers her e-mail, so she probably won't show up for shoots."

3)   Use "bcc" when sending out mass solicitations. That's "blind carbon copy." Reading an individual piece of e-mail won't give away all the other addresses it was sent to. If you write the message well, each recipient will believe it was sent just to them.

4)   Think before you hit the "send" button. It's cathartic to write a nasty response to someone who has been less than professional with you, but do you really want to start a flame war with potential employers? So, they're jerks. Erase the strong language and tell them simply, "We can't come to an agreement at this time, sorry." Take the high road and move on.

5)   Use proper grammar and spelling. It will separate you from the pack and make you stand out in a good way. Don't use "txt msg" shortcuts, 'leetspeak, or urban slang. Business requires precise communication, especially when conducted via e-mail.

Telephone:

I strongly recommend TracFone as a business line. Many of the models I've worked with either had a TracFone, or switched to one after I talked with them about it. Again, as with e-mail addresses, have a phone you use strictly for your business, and give that number out via profiles and on your cards. You should have another phone number you give to Grandma.

With TracFone (or other pay-as-you-go wireless services), you'll be charged by the minute, and occasionally need to buy refill minutes. While that may not seem economical, remember: this is a business tool, and that's all. It's used to talk with producers. Don't use it for text messaging, sending nude pix of yourself, or anything else the phone will do. Those services will chew up your pre-paid minutes, and at some crucial point where you're stuck in East Bumfuck with no way to pay for minutes, making that career-defining appointment with one of the Big Boys, you're going to regret sending a bunch of grainy phone pix to some wankmeister who isn't going to hire you anyway. Get a phone with the least number of features you can find, and use it only for talking with producers.

Take some time to write a professional sounding voice mail message. If you don't have a friend who can help you produce a professional voice message, that's okay. Just practice saying the message yourself, and record it though your phone. Whatever you do, DO NOT play music from a boom box or radio before, during or after your message. Take my word, it does not make you sound professional, it makes you sound like a 12 year old girl. It sounds like crap.

Here's a suggested 30 second script for your voice message. Obviously, you'll put in the information that's specific to you:

> *Hello! You've reached Gwen Kix, model and actress. I'm based in Muncie, Indiana, but am currently traveling the East coast of the US. I'm booking paid shoots only at this time. For lingerie, glamour, fitness and art nudes, I'm your model. I'm looking for opportunities in stills and video, but I don't do explicit content. Visit my web site at www.GwenKixModel.com for stats and booking info. Find my sample stills and references on the major portfolio sites. My OneModelPlace ID is OU812, and my ModelGig number is EIEIO99. Producers, please leave your name, contact information and shoot details at the tone. Thanks for calling!*

Snail Mail:

Whether it's in your home town, or some place you pass through on a regular basis, invest in a PO box, or maybe even one from one of the private mail services. My box is in a mall, so I can get in and grab my mail late at night.

What will you get via snail mail? Many model profile sites insist on you supplying a mailing address. Maybe they'll send you a tee shirt and some bumper stickers. You can list it on model releases without fear of having some whacko show up outside your window some night. I've seen plenty of drivers' licenses with PO Boxes as the model's legal address. You can list it for fans to send you gifts if you dare, although I don't recommend that. It's another way of staying in contact, while giving yourself some privacy and security.

Business Cards:

Yes, you need these. When you come face-to-face with anyone in the industry, slap a card in their hand. When you drop a thank-you note in the mail to a producer or another model, drop one in the envelope. Yes, you gave them one before, but business cards tend to get lost, or used as book-marks or toothpicks.

At the very least, your card should contain all the contact info we've gone over here. It also doesn't hurt to have a short line on there about the type of work you're looking for, or that you specialize in.

Comp cards & Head shots:

Comp Cards:
Also called zed cards. These are printed cards with several of the model's photos, her vital statistics, and contact information.
Two most popular sizes are: 8.5" x 5.5" and 8" x 10".

Most often, you'll hand these out to directly to pro-ducers, or to the advertising client. Lots of room for additional information, either on the front (people are lazy) or sometimes the back. I've gotten two, I think, in the years I've been shooting content. I would use these as a follow-up to phone conversation or e-mail exchange where a job you really want is down be-tween you and one or two other people. They're a bit too expensive to send out in a shotgun approach to finding a job. After all, we've been talking about how the Internet is faster and cheaper. But sometimes, an 8 x 10 comp card coming in the mail is just the right way to introduce yourself to a potential employer.

Postcards

I really recommend having a stack of postcards created from the best of your work. You promote yourself and your favorite photog at the same time. But remember, the pictures can be seen by anyone, so try to keep them more artistic and less risque'.

The cards themselves can take the place of the larger head shot prints, you can put more info on the back, and they cost a hell of a lot less to mail. Best of all, the recipient can tack your picture up on the wall without hav-ing to open an envelope.

While these are less expensive all around, I still don't recommend you send these out willy-nilly. Use them for major updates – adding a new con-tent niche to your repertoire, changing your address, updating your phone number, or something similar. Remember the boy who cried wolf. Send special mailings too often, and when you really have something important to say, your card may end up in the trash.

CASHING IN

This chapter covers a couple things: getting paid for your work, and getting paid for your work *again*. Yup, there are several ways you can keep getting paid for being in front of the camera, long after the shoot. I've seen models get paid years after doing a shoot!

First things first – getting paid for your shoot. In order to get paid, you'll probably have to provide the producer with copies of two forms of ID showing your legal name. At least one of them should be government issued with your photo on it – a driver's license, passport, an Under-21 ID card, etc. You can use almost anything as the 2nd ID as long as it has the same name on it. I've had women try to give me their credit cards – don't do it. I'm fairly honest, but don't put temptation in my path. Never give another person access to any of your financial information unless you're making a secure transaction, and you can make sure they don't keep any extra copies of the information.

Most small producers will pay you at the end of the shoot, usually in cash. Producers who are shooting you for a major market, and paying more money, will also want your Social Security number (so they can report the payment to the IRS – I told you to be legal!), and may pay you with a company issued check. Always verify payment terms when setting up the shoot. Don't wait until you get there. If the producer asks to pay you by check (or says it's "Company Policy"), ask which bank the check will be drawn on. This is why it's important to have an account with a bank that services the area where you'll be shooting. My tiny home-town bank is very friendly, but I don't pay models from another state with a check from there. Banks don't like to cash checks for people who aren't depositors – they can't verify that the issuer actually wrote the check, and they want a way to at least try to get the money back if they get scammed. If you do get a check, the bank name and phone number should be on the front of it. It doesn't hurt to call and verify the full amount of the check is available before you try to deposit it.

In the early stages of your career, it's very unlikely (although not impossible) that you'll be working for a major producer. A very few producers expect to send you a check at some later date. These are the types of shoots that are usually set up by an agent, and the agent gets the check.

61

They then turn around and pay you or your business manager. For most beginning models, you can expect to be paid immediately after the shoot.

Another way to get paid is by credit card. In order to do this, you'll need some kind of account that can process the cards for you. PayPal is one service that can take cards for you. However, some people have experienced trouble with their accounts, and PayPal's Terms Of Service (TOS) specifically prohibit paying − or receiving payment − for illegal activities. They also don't like you using your account to transact for obscenity and pornography, although I've seen them turn a blind eye. You can bill a producer for "On site modeling services" or some such, without explaining exactly what that is to PayPal. There are a number of other services similar to PayPal that have no restrictions against adult product and services. However, PayPal (owned by eBay) is the biggest player.

I've never used them, but I understand from some models that they've been paid with pre-paid debit cards. If you can verify the amount on the card, and use them somewhere where you're not going to be charged a service fee, I see no problem with that. I really have no experience with them − I'd ask around before accepting them.

Cash, as they say, is king. You can buy a banker's pen for just a few dollars at almost any office supply store. Swipe these pens across the bills, and you can verify that the bills are real or counterfeit. The instructions are usually on the back of the pack. Not that a producer paying you in cash is deliberately trying to pass off a bad bill, but they're human too, and can get scammed just as easily as you. Better to verify that the bills are real before having your bank refuse a big hunk of your pay as fake.

If you're the adventurous sort, you may be willing to accept something else of value for your time, instead of cash or one of it's many replacements. I've given models gift certificates to restaurants, for instance. I know some that have accepted airline tickets, store gift cards, and personal photographic instruction. One model I know of got a used car for an afternoon of shooting. It ran for about six months, and then died, but if you think about it, the car lasted a hell of a lot longer than the cash would have. She was able to get to a lot more shoots and make cash, so she was happy, too.

Depending on the content you've helped create, getting paid again for your work might be pretty easy. Unless you posed for a producer who's simply working on his own portfolio, they're probably using your image (stills, video or both) for a larger project on which they expect to make money. A book, a video, a paid-access web site. . . any of these is an opportunity for you to make more money on your shoot.

How? By helping promote and sell the final product!

The first way you can do this is by asking to be considered for personal appearances. If the photographer is using your images in an upcoming book, tell them you'd love to do a signing with him at a local book store. I'd pitch the producer a low appearance fee, plus a dollar amount for each book sold at the signing. Make sure it's okay with the photog, and offer to sign one of the pictures of you for the book buyer. People come out of the woodwork for signed books, especially if it's got more than one signature. You can do the same thing for a DVD, or even a fine-art showing. It never hurts to ask, and since your appearance will help them make money, I can't see why they'd decline. Of course, once the appearance is set up, do everything in your power to promote it. Send an e-mail to all your fans, and to other producers in the area. If you have a following in another geographic area, try to get the producer to come out there with you and do another signing.

Money Talks

Helping producers make money makes you valuable to them.

Tactfully point out that you'd love it if they spent some of the money you helped them make on hiring you for more work.

Appearing in person is great, but how about using the technology you've got at your fingertips? The Internet is one big shopping mall. I shudder to think of the extreme ranges of products and services that can be bought and sold via the 'net. But it certainly helps you out.

E-commerce is essentially buying and selling things over the 'net, using the digital exchange of monetary information to pass payment back and forth – usually with credit or debit cards. Most producers have someone else collecting money for them, a large company that specializes in handling cash on the 'net. Some require that the exchange be for a physical product, like a book or DVD. Some handle the funds for paid access web sites, where your photos or videos are behind a secure area, and people pay to get access to them. Most of these large processors have something called "affiliate programs." That is, you can sign up with the processor, and for every sale you help make you get a percentage of the sale.

If the producer has books or DVDs for sale on, say, Amazon, you can sign up as an Amazon affiliate and advertise them from you web site. You can even advertise products in which you don't appear. You can promote anything you like, and some people make a lot of money as affiliates for certain on-line e-commerce sites. But I'd use it as a sideline for your modeling career – something to make cash at 4 AM while you're asleep.

If the producer has a pay site, he's probably using one of a handful of credit card processors as the "gatekeeper" to the digital content he has for sale. Most of these processors live and die by their affiliate programs. The more people they can get to promote the sites for which they collect funds. . . the more funds there are to collect. If you're posing for content that will appear on some type of pay site, ask the producer about joining his affiliate program, and helping him promote his site. If he doesn't have one, strongly suggest that he set one up with his existing processor, or switch to one that allows affiliates. The more money he makes, the more money you make. If someone wants to see your stills or video, that's great. If they want to see someone else, that's great too, as long as you both make money.

In very simplistic terms, an affiliate program works like this: the processor gives you an ID number, which is kind of like a digital ticket. You create a link to the product or site from your web site (or anywhere else, for that matter), making sure to include the digital ticket. I come along and decide I want to see more of you, so I click on the link and a copy of this digital ticket gets stuck to my forehead (figuratively). This link actually goes to the payment processor, but they re-direct me to the content or product I was looking for. If I decide to buy the book, or pay to join the web site, the processor sees the ticket that's on my forehead, and splits the payment I make three ways: a percentage for them, a percentage for the seller, and one for you. That amount goes into your account, and when they make sure I'm not going to make a charge-back, my payment will get pooled with the rest of the commissions you've made and you'll get your money.

You need to stay on top of the sites run by the producers you work with, to make sure they're still there and still working with the same payment processor. But depending on how many pay sites and book/video producers you work with, this could be a major source of additional income. By spending just a couple hours each week, you could conceivably continue to make money on one shoot for years and years.

MANAGING YOUR INCOME

If you've taken my advice on setting yourself up as a business, you'll be setting aside money to pay your taxes. Now you can go out and blow the rest!

Wait... not so fast. Here are some things you need to do with your income before you go on a spending spree.

1) PAY YOUR BUSINESS EXPENSES: If you're running a tab for anything related to the business of modeling, make a payment. If you have a gas card or business credit card, pay it off at the end of each month. If you use a pre-paid phone, pre-paid gas card, train or bus passes, anything like that – consider "topping it off" by making a payment.

2) PAY HEALTH RELATED EXPENSES: If modeling is your primary job, buy medical insurance, and set up a Health Savings Account (HSA). If you do have a "day job" where you get insurance and benefits, that's great. Talk with a financial advisor – you might want or need extra insurance.

Once you've gotten your current and future medical and dental bills covered, consider joining a gym, or some other type of health club or service. Learning a martial art and training in it several times per week will give you double benefits: keeping you fit, and teaching you self defense techniques.

3) GET A MEMBERSHIP WITH AAA: If you travel to and from shoots in your own car, this is a no-brainer. What many people don't realize is that AAA memberships are no longer tied to a specific automobile, but to a member's card. That means if you carpool to a shoot with someone else your membership applies if their car breaks down.

I shot a model a few years ago who had a blow-out on the NY State Thruway on the way home. Between myself and two other producers, she'd made more that $700 cash that day. After towing expenses, a new tire, and a hotel room with late check-out, she had $50 in her purse when she got home. At least some of those expenses could have been less painful if she'd had a AAA card.

AAA membership also gets you discounts on everything from hotel rooms to eye glasses. Even a 10% discount is better than a sharp stick in the eye, as they say.

An added benefit? Use your AAA card as your second form of ID on shoots.

4) KEEP YOUR CAR IN GOOD SHAPE: Keep your car insured with a good company. Change the oil on a regular basis. Keep the best possible tires on it, and keep them inflated. Keep the car washed and waxed, and clean out the accumulated road trash every chance you get. Make repairs as soon as possible. An automobile in good shape will get you to shoots on time, and in comfort. Keeping your vehicle in top shape is a good investment.

5) PRE-PAY YOUR PROMOTIONAL EXPENSES: Many web hosts and site designers will give you a discount if you pay several months in advance, topping out at about 1 year. Contact your Internet service provider (ISP) and phone service – see if they offer pre-payment discounts. If you can't get a discount, ask for bonus products or services for pre-paying.

Just because you're using the 'net to find work doesn't mean printed promotional shots are a bad idea. On the contrary – dropping a new head shot to a producer you've worked with before can lead to additional work. Sending them to producers you want to work with should be on your to-do list as well. Buy them in bulk and save. Carry them like business cards and hand them out like candy.

6) PLAN FOR THE FUTURE – SET UP A RETIREMENT ACCOUNT: Set aside a few bucks from each shoot. Every month, or more often if you can, put that money somewhere you can't touch it. Set up an IRA (Individual Retirement Account) or SEP (Self Employment Pension) through a financial advisor or, if you feel daring, invest directly in stocks. Like many other things I've mentioned, a complete discussion of financial planning is beyond (way beyond!) the scope of this book. See the notes after the last chapter.

7) KEEP IN TOUCH WITH FRIENDS AND FAMILY: Some models get so focused on the business aspect they forget that it is people who

make life worth living. And the most important people are the ones who supported you "way back when."

Yes, we live in an age of instantaneous communication. Cell phones and the Internet bring most parts of the globe within reach.

But as you travel, send back post cards, souvenirs, trinkets – anything and everything. And make sure you include a piece of yourself, some reference to your relationship with that person. A blog or mass e-mail cannot help you maintain personal relationships with the important people in your life.

Do all of these things, and then you can – and should – spend money on yourself. I know a couple models who were making a lot of money, and sending most of it back home. The one who sent every extra penny back for her sister's health care quickly came to resent the job, the producers, the other models. . . and her sister. The other model occasionally splurged on herself. A fancy dinner here, a day at the spa there, a new pair of comfy running shoes. She lasted quite a bit longer, and enjoyed her time as a model until she quit the business to stay at home and raise a family.

HEALTHY ———▶ WEALTHY

The most obvious reason to stay healthy is: if you're too sick to work, you can't make money. Money invested wisely eventually leads to wealth. Investing in your health is pretty smart.

So, how do you stay (or become) healthy so that you can get wealthy? Your mind and body need to work together to keep your entire self healthy.

Lifestyle

Mentally, you need to embrace the idea that staying healthy is a process you incorporate into your lifestyle. It's not easy – if it were, everyone would automatically do it and there'd be no reason to read (or even write) this chapter. It takes self-discipline, the mental strength to both resist unhealthy influences and to make yourself do the healthy things. It's easy to find excuses not to do them.

You should begin by eliminating and avoiding negative influences. Illicit and illegal drug use not only damages your body, it erodes your self-discipline and judgment, making bad choices seem good.

A positive mental attitude is essential as well. Not only do you need to grow a "Yes I can" mind set, you need to quit listening to Negative Nellies. You know these people – they don't have a positive thing to say about you, themselves, or anyone else. Psychological studies show that we are influenced by the attitudes around us.

Eliminating bad influences from your life is a good start. You also need to add positive things back in.

Exercise programs not only help keep your body healthy, they increase blood flow through the brain, allowing you to think better. Continued learning strengthens your mental abilities, helping develop self-esteem from overcoming challenges and learning objectives.

Physical

Some things are okay for your body in moderation: rest, calories and alcohol, for instance. Other things like tobacco and recreational drug use should be eliminated.

Once you eliminate the negative habits, you need to replace them with positive ones. Make a habit of taking a good quality multi-vitamin each day. Replace eating excess food with making it – spend time preparing your own healthy meals. Can't boil water? An evening cooking class is better for you than Seinfeld re-runs anyway.

Snacking on fruit gives lots of benefits at once: water, fiber, sugars for energy. Much better than the empty calories from chips and candy.

Drinking water helps fill you up, and is beneficial for flushing waste out of your body's cells. Since our bodies are made up mostly of water, drinking plenty of liquids each day will also keep you feeling better.

A well rounded exercise program will keep your muscles strong, and your limbs and joints flexible. You'll find this helpful when called upon to contort yourself into unnatural positions, like having your head and butt point the same direction, and then staying there while they get just the right shot. Building up your strength will also help when you're forced to carry a fifty-pound bag of clothes and make-up up three flights of stairs in an unused warehouse for a shoot.

I know several models who practice one or more of the martial arts, although pilates and yoga are beneficial as well. Side benefits of learning a martial art include better balance, more self confidence, and the self determination to walk away from a situation where you might get assaulted before it happens. Also, if somebody makes unwanted physical advances, you can kick their ass.

Physical training can also lead to muscular definition, or "cuts." Definition plus lights equals shadow, and shadows make for more interesting and dramatic photos. You don't have to look like a weight lifter for the definition to become apparent.

Being physically fit allows you to see, do and learn more as well. Imagine being able to help carry equipment to the top of a cliff and watching a spectacular sunrise or sunset as the producer shoots you against it. Being in shape has many, many benefits.

Mental

Slumped on your sofa watching re-runs is not only bad for you physically, it stunts your ability to think. Like physical exercise, mental exercise is beneficial as well. Taking classes on various subjects will make you more desirable to producers, since you'll be able to more easily fit into various situations (knowing how to handle chemistry equipment, or being able to speak French, for instance). It also keeps your mind nimble, helps you think on your feet. Also, in our increasingly information-centric society, the more you know, the more power and influence you have.

Many women who get into the darker aspects of adult Internet modeling have issues they need to work out. To be fair, we all do. But my point is that you can take control of your life only by having mental strength, and you can move from an attitude of "I can't do anything but this," to one of "I'll do what I want to do, and make money at it" only with self determination and resolve. Your success or failure at this or any other career is completely within your own power.

Mental strength allows you to negotiate better, make better choices, help give positive advice to others, and in general have a better life. Literally thousands of books have been written on developing mental and emotional strength. If books don't work for you, there are many psychologists and therapists around the country that might be able to help you out. If you've followed the advice in the earlier chapters, you've set yourself up with insurance. With that, and the fact that you should be making a good income, should allow you to afford the best therapist for you, if you decide you need one. There's no longer any social stigma associated with seeing a therapist, so don't let the thought your friends will find out keep you from going.

Mental strength is essential, because your mind controls your body. With mental strength, you can make your body do what you need it to.

Mental strength also allows you to put aside money in a savings account when you'd rather buy a new car stereo, or spend it on something else.

Wealth

Wealth is not entirely the same as "riches." You can be rich without being wealthy. Being rich is having a lot of money in your pocket. Wealth is money, along with the will power and wisdom to invest it, to keep it growing itself, and to keep it working for you instead of the other way around.

<table>
<tr><td>

Master Mind

In his book *Think And Grow Rich*, author Napoleon Hill recommended joining a master mind group.

Members of a master mind group are dedicated to achieving the same goals, and keeping each other focused and motivated.

Visit www.AdultModleingBook/mm to join ours.

</td><td>

Most people in America are within two paychecks of losing their lives. If they were to lose their jobs, most families would be on the streets in weeks. Think about how many times you've heard (or thought) "I need that money so I can pay my rent this month." Money – cash, coin, moolah – is just a tool. You need a hammer to drive a nail, and you need cash to pay your rent. Being wealthy is having a different mind set, as well as having money. Most of the people around you are working for today. Rich people blow money on stuff, like houses, watches, and sports cars. How many celebrities have you read about that used to be famous, and are now broke? Sure, sometimes their money was embezzled by former associates, but a lot of their bankruptcy is both monetary and mental. If you put another several million dollars in their hands, it would be gone again in no time.

</td></tr>
</table>

There are three deceptively simple keys to wealth.

❖Working for the future, instead of for today
❖Investing your money, instead of spending or
   saving it
❖Caring and acting for others

At first, you're just scrambling to make money. That's understandable. But you need to develop the wealth mindset fairly quickly.

Working for the future means setting personal and financial goals and working toward them. It means forgoing expensive dinners every night now so that in the future, when you can't - or have decided not to - work, you can eat then. It's spending money on a dependable car now so that you can make more money and buy a flashy one later on, when you can enjoy it more. It's putting money into a retirement account, even though you really want those new shoes.

Investing is taking money, and putting it to work. There are as many books on investing as there are on mental health. You can buy into a business, or buy property, or build your own business doing something else. Investing is putting your money back into a money-making venture and taking a risk that it will succeed. Saving is putting your money in a bank, or under your mattress. Returns from investments are based on risk - the more you risk, the greater the reward you want there to be. However, investing and managing risk is not the same as gambling! Again, this subject is too involved for a book on modeling, but it is important. Do your own research, and talk to your financial advisors.

A very important key to being wealthy is *thinking about others, and acting on their behalf.* That can be as simple as making donations to charities. You can spend time and money building houses for the homeless. You can take your knowledge and experience and teach people a skill or craft. The idea is to give back to the less fortunate in some way. Make sure your efforts and money benefit them more physically than they do you, and you'll become very wealthy both mentally and emotionally.

Wealth is having money, your health, and time enough to enjoy both.

FETISH BAG

When anthropologists talk about "fetish objects" they're talking about things that people believe have special, supernatural powers. An example would be a small doll, made in the "image" of a goddess, carried around to help protect the person from harm or other gods. In the mind of the person holding it, a fetish object takes on all the powers of the original item.

This is where the understanding of sexual fetishism comes from. "Normal sex" (if there is such a thing) is all about putting Tab A into Slot B, and that's it. But if, for instance, a person becomes sexually excited by leather boots instead of the otherwise naked woman wearing them, a psychologist would call this sexual (or erotic) fetishism. Thankfully for both therapists and creators of erotic content, there's no shortage of fetishes or the people who want them fulfilled.

I've personally shot fetish material that other people got very excited about, and yet I have no clue why. Popping balloons with your ass, or stepping on food or stuffed animals. . . it doesn't turn me on in the least. But if people pay, and I can keep from laughing on tape, I'll shoot it. As I said before, I have a friend who shoots rope bondage content with some of the same models I've used. If I tried to shoot that content with the same models, people wouldn't like it. Why? My knots are poor quality. It's not the naked woman tied up on the floor that turns them on, it's seeing her struggle against ropes and knots that the viewer knows are difficult of get out of. They're looking at the ropes dig into her skin, watching her muscles straining against the tight bonds.

Almost anything can be a fetish. The more prevalent fetishes are foot, leather, and bondage. There are always people shooting content for these. It's the smaller, micro-niche fetishes that really pay, though. There are fewer people who produce it, because there are fewer people buying it. I used to shoot videos for a collector named Bob. He'd send me scripts and script outlines, and I'd shoot them. I'd act out his part behind the camera, and the model would repeatedly call me "Bob." Over and over. And over. I mean like three times every sentence. Since the name is fairly common, I made a deal with him that I could resell the tapes. He loved them, and I and my models would break into gales of laughter when talking about doing yet another Bob movie.

There are many fetishes where you can keep within whatever limits you've set for yourself, and still make some serious cash. One of my friend's regular models, Ginger, will not appear without panties. However, she's very willing to have her augmented breasts groped and squeezed while she's tied up, or "being abducted." Actually, costumes can be a big component of fetishes. Think nurses, librarians, soldiers, cops, business people and the ever-popular Catholic school girl outfit. Other adult fetishes include smoking, bondage, humiliation, voyeurism, adult babies, breath manipulation and spanking, all of which can be done in various stages of dress and undress.

Voyeurism:

Sexual stimulation coming from watching others, especially when they don't know you're watching.

Watched content can be sexually stimulating without being sexual itself.

I know some models who only perform in fetish content. If you specialize in making a certain type of content and get to know exactly what your customers are looking for, you can make quite a good living. Some models will do catalog work (appearing in advertisements holding kitchen gizmos in department store fliers, for instance) and then change their look completely and appear as crop wielding demonesses commanding you scum – Yes, you! - to get on your knees and lick their boots.

The oddest fetish I know of has to do (outwardly, anyway) with shrinking. The camera starts off level with the model, and then she slips "you" a drink, or kisses "you" on the lips with poisoned lipstick, and you begin to shrink. "Your" clothes start dropping off as you become too small to wear them, until the camera is looking up at this giantess from the level of her feet. This is where the verbal humiliation kicks in to compliment the visual cues that the viewer is much too insignificant for her respect and attraction. Intellectually, I get it. Sexually, I'm extremely boring. With my upbringing, you'd think I had a whole host of weird experiences to sexualize, but I'm actually very vanilla.

There are certain fetishes you have to be careful about, though. The crush fetish is often about seeing a powerful or careless woman crush bugs, worms, and small animals to death under her shoes. I don't condone that anyway, but this type of content is now illegal, and crush fans are now forced to watch food (pudding, gelatin, mashed potatoes – anything that's easily squished) and small stuffed animals tortured under foot. Many hard-core abuse videos now have a short segment at the end where the abused talent sits with her abuser, laughing and happy, and talks about what a turn-on the whole fantasy role-play experience has been. Otherwise, it's automatically assumed that the woman was forced into being abused. And breath control abuse, either by constricting the airway (choking) or by making the person hold their own breath (face under water) can be dangerous. If you're doing that, always make sure there's someone on-hand who's trained in lifesaving and first aid.

Almost anything is a turn-on for someone out there. A lot of fashion and art photography is filled with erotically fetishistic images, so before you look down your nose at doing "fetish porn," look at the type of high-brow material already being produced by the people you aspire to work with. I say if they're paying, let's make it!

LET'S TALK ABOUT PORN

There can be no meaningful book about adult modeling without a frank and open discussion of pornography. Even if you find this topic offensive, I suggest you read this chapter. Why? Because knowledge is power. If you refuse to do this type of content, you'll at least know why you refuse.

"Pornography" is from the Greek, meaning "whore pictures." It was a word used to describe the graphic advertisements for various sex acts, drawn by prostitutes (or their agents) to lure in customers. That's right – the world's oldest profession directly spawned another profession almost equally as reviled – the ad man.

Porn is concerned with the "primary external sexual organs" - genitalia. The penis, the vagina, and all the ways they can be shown in action. In primates, our genitalia are hidden away from our own eyes, beneath our torsos and between limbs that, in general, don't open that far apart. Human genitalia are figuratively shrouded in mystery, and literally shrouded in shadow.

Since porn focuses on the genitalia during various sex acts, from solo masturbation to group copulation, it requires light – lots and lots of light. Specifically, well-lit genitalia.

According to ex porn star and adult magazine publisher Gloria Leonard, light is the main difference between pornography and it's kissing cousin, erotica. Pornography has well-lit crotches in action.

I'm not going to try to talk you into shooting porn. Then again, I'm not going to try to talk you out of it. However, there are a number of issues "behind the scenes" that casual observers aren't aware of, and that you should at least hear about before making a decision.

First is the money. The latest figures show that porn in all its forms, whether it's on-line, in print, or video, is a multi-billion (with a "B") industry in the US. For all the noise about how it's an immoral, sexist, corrupting influence, we sure are making and buying a lot of it. There are couples having sex on Internet video streams and charging people all over the county an arm and a leg to see their arms and legs - and other body parts.

The flow of money touches several different jobs in the porn industry. The one you're most interested in is the on-camera talent. Then there are the people who package the raw images and footage, and put them into a product (video, web site, magazine, etc.) that people buy. There are distributors of physical product, and people who market any or all of it. On the web, there are affiliate programs where any enterprising person can make money just by leading people to adult web sites. There are the people who host web sites, duplicate DVDs, and print magazines. There are scouts who go looking for new talent. And finally, there are the credit card processing companies that collect all the virtual dollars from the individuals who have to have their porn. Here's a not-so-secret secret: the more you can do yourself, the more money you keep. If you shoot yourself, you don't have to pay talent. Put together your own web site, promote your content, and sell it yourself, and you can keep the money from all those steps from flowing to other people.

On the other hand, there's a reason why jobs have specialists who do them. Poorly lit content promoted via a bad looking web site just doesn't sell very well, and you may wind up losing money rather than actually making it.

Pornography has become more increasingly mainstream, with starlets crossing over first from blue films into rock videos, and then into feature films and television. There is also the "reverse crossover" where celebrities have had their private sex tapes leaked, and even created "accidental" leaks that were calculated to reinvigorate their flagging career. Ordinary folks have become minor celebrities when their private videos and images have been made public through accidental loss, or by jealous ex-lovers circulating the material.

In the US, the commercial porn industry is still centered in what has been called "Silicone Valley" both for it's location in California near the so-called Silicon Valley, and the sheer number of porn starlets sporting breast implants. But with the advent of the Internet and cheaper, high-quality video equipment, anyone can become an amateur porn producer with very little investment. However, in most areas of the country, the cops who watch it in their patrol cars will arrest your ass for shooting or distributing it.

Aside from moral issues, there are medical issues. With all the attention it's garnered in the last 25 years, AIDS is still a concern. But people tend to forget about the "common" diseases like syphilis, gonorrhea, genital warts, herpes and hepatitis. There are a lot of misconceptions out there about who can get sick, how and with what. While a complete discussion of sexual health issues is far beyond the scope of this book, I find it frankly amazing how a person who will drop their clothes on camera and perform sex acts for an audience of millions is too embarrassed to visit a doctor to talk about their sexual health in private.

Let me just say that if you're in porn, or considering it, get an AIMS (Adult Industry Medical STD) test. If you wind up in porn, get them often. Actually, it's a good idea to talk with your health care provider about your sexual health, even if you're in a monogamous relationship. I once shuttled a college co-ed to the hospital because she'd passed out from pain "down there." She'd never been to a gynecologist because her mother said only "dirty people need to do that." Luckily there was nothing seriously wrong, but there could have been. Don't let your life become the punchline of a joke: "She literally died from embarrassment."

You will also find some seriously damaged people in porn – perhaps more than in almost any other industry. Those with self-esteem problems, mental illness and truckloads of emotional baggage find it very easy and lucrative to get a job having sex in front of others.

That said, in pornography there is someone for just about everyone. People who like to be spanked and humiliated will find people who like to spank and humiliate. People who need a constant stream of new sexual partners will find the revolving door to porn supplying them with new partners hourly. People who get no respect elsewhere can become famous for the very qualities that make normal society shun them: obesity, tiny genitals, excess body hair, dwarfism – almost any bodily condition can become a fetish (see the Fetish Bag chapter).

There are even production niches for people who already have herpes, or who are HIV positive, to perform on camera with those similarly afflicted.

Most performers in porn find their career life cycle to be very short. The main reason is that they got in to make some quick cash, and then got out again. Others, who want to continue on, haven't applied the techniques you now know from reading this book, and wind up working in the fast food industry instead. You can literally work for two weeks straight, quit the industry, and have "new material" surface for the next 18 months. There is very little footage that winds up "on the cutting room floor" in porn. Over 100 years ago, they were the first industry to embrace the green philosophy: reduce, reuse, recycle.

But the public's great desire for new material means that if you manage your career the right way, treat it as a business, and keep your head on straight, you could enjoy a lucrative run in pornography. If you walk in with other experience under your belt in niche content, adult nudes, and such, you'll have the ability to work with the producers on a more equal basis.

The pornography side of the adult Internet modeling business can be scary, and it can be seductive. If you are not 110% sure you want to be in it, then stay away from it. If you do decide you want to perform in porn, it's important you have friends (and maybe family) who know what you're doing and support your decision. In the Business chapter, I talked about the importance of planning. In porn, the most important part of your plan is the exit strategy. While not exactly porn, Sydney Barrows - famous in the 1980's as New York City's Mayflower Madam - was busted. She went on to become a best selling author and highly regarded sales consultant. Today, current porn stars are writing autobiographies and novels, and going on to become mainstream actors and actresses.

Exit Strategy

Smart business people have a plan in place on how to leave their business.

Set your goals early, and plan how to transition when you decide to stop modeling. A definite exit plan will save you worry and heartache.

CULTIVATE CELEBRITY

There is a special area of promotion that, by it's nature, is almost self-perpetuating. Once you get this ball rolling, it says rolling through it's own momentum.

Celebrity.

Celebrity is part of the larger, umbrella concept of "fame." There are many reasons a person can be known as a celebrity. There are several young women who have created a sub-class of celebrity: the "celebutantes." These are young women with too much time and too much money. I see no reason to name them here, but you know who they are. They are famous for being famous. When they get caught on tape doing something stupid, illegal or both, that only adds to their notoriety.

While I don't encourage you to become like them completely, understanding how they continue to garner attention is worth examining.

First, as I said, they're famous for being famous. This is a tough principle to kick-start. Unless you're born to wealth, royalty or fame, you have to make this a follow-up principle, rather than the initial one.

So how do you get to be famous? Be seen with famous people. Get your picture taken with them. Be associated with them, and have them mention you to other people. This is classic coattail promotion, taken straight from the old movie studio system. In order to promote an unknown starlet, you set her up on a date with a leading man and made sure the newshounds knew where to find them.

Another cliché from the days of the movie studio: have yourself paged in a hotel full of important people. Make sure the powerful hear your name, over and over again.

> **Cult Of Personality**
>
> A term often attributed to the larger-than-life public images created for the leaders - especially dictators - of countries.
>
> Some celebrities feel they *must* be the center of attention, and do everything possible to create a cult of personality for themselves.

While we have more sophisticated ways of self promotion today, including the Internet, fax and e-mail campaigns, there is something to be said for the low-tech, old fashioned techniques.

When you meet someone more famous than yourself, ask them if they'd pose for a photo. Since "perception is reality," and you are known for the company you keep, getting photographed with a famous person helps a little bit of their fame rub off on you. You can then use these photos in your own publicity campaigns.

Somewhat more difficult for those who are humble and quiet by nature, is creating your own celebrity. By that I mean a sort of self-aggrandizing posturing that helps propel your name, and the image you want to promote, into the minds of your potential audience.

The problem with this technique is that, unfortunately, some people come to believe their own hype. You must always remember that this persona is very much like a mask – or even a full-body costume – you wear out in public. For promotional purposes, Halloween lasts all year long..

When notices go out about your appearances, or about a particular accomplishment, they can be simple statements of fact, which may get you noticed. Or they can contain celebrity-inducing items. Here are two examples for the same news item.

Example 1

Gwen Kix, nationally known bikini model, will sign copies of her calendar at MegaBooks this Saturday from noon to 3 PM.

Example 2

Gwen Kix, whose bikini-modeling video had the most downloads on BlooToob for the month of July, will be signing copies of her calendar at MegaBooks this Saturday from noon to 3 PM. Kix, national spokesperson for Canine Nasal Congestion Research, is donating all proceeds from calendar sales to the charity, and will appear with Charlie the Stuffy Puppy, the charity's mascot.

The first example catches the attention of people who have an interest in the model, and in the book store. The second additionally trades on video downloads, charity in general, this charity in particular, and people who like puppies. And any personal appearance may allow the Great Unwashed Masses to pose with Someone Famous.

Speaking of charities, becoming the spokesperson for one is a great way to cycle up your celebrity. It gives you entree to other celebrities, good press, and a legitimate reason to have your name and photo spread throughout the media.

I really don't suggest this, but I understand that there are certain attention starved individuals in Hollywood who have two publicists: one sends out good news, and one leaks terrible rumors which the celebrity must then refute on a national talk show. Effective? Maybe. Sad? Definitely.

WRAP-UP

As a photographer, I need something to shoot. My favorite subject? The nude female form. I'd be nowhere without the hundreds of women who have appeared in front of my lenses. I appreciate all the established models who have worked with me over the years, and I'm grateful for having the opportunity to work with many, many first-time models. Some have appeared nude, and some with more clothing on. Either way, I've learned quite a great deal by helping to teach them the business. So I thank them as well.

As a first-time author, I'd certainly be out a great deal of time and effort if there was no-one reading this book. So to all of you who are looking to make a better life for yourselves, and who took a chance on that by purchasing this book (or borrowing it from a friend), I thank you as well.

Together, we've gone though a great deal of information. I hope you've learned something. More importantly, I hope you take that knowledge and apply it to your own efforts at becoming a successful adult Internet model. There were several additional subjects I wanted to cover, but I just didn't have the time to get them done before the deadline. If the book sells well, and the feedback is positive enough, maybe I'll go back and add more information.

For those of you who are serious about adult Internet modeling, please keep an eye out for the companion workbook. From personal experience in seeing what other models have done, it's not an exaggeration to say that you can make a six-figure income from doing this, and have a great time doing it as well. The workbook is your second step in getting there, after this book.

Please visit the web site, www.AdultModelingBook.com and read more information as we make it available. In addition, we'll be adding a member's only area in the future. Make sure you join, and interact with all the other models who are reading this book.

A quick thanks to Scott Gardner of Agile' Marketing Services. He took our discussions and my notes, and made this into a real book. Agile' is also hosting, designing and running the web site. They're good folks - hire them.

On the web site, we offer a place for you to ask questions and make comments and suggestions. Please join us there - we'd love to hear from you!

No single book can contain all the information about a subject. And every book has a "point of view" - this one certainly does. It covers the way I've experienced the business, and how I see it. If you've had different experiences, I hope you won't think I've tried to lie and scam my way through writing a book. I've just provided my own personal point of view.

Thank you all again! I look forward to seeing some of you in front of my lens!

Very Best,

Tony Perfect

RESOURCES

Portfolio Web Sites

www.ModelMayhem.com

www.SexyJobs.com

www.MuseCube.com

www.BabeWarehouse.com

www.FreelanceModels.com

www.OneModelPlace.com

www.AllModelZone.com

www.ModelOverdrive.com

www.GlamourModels.com

www.GarageGlamour.com

www.Models.com

www.ModelGig.com

www.HardCoreModeling.com

Books Of Interest

Stay Mad For Life – Jim Cramer
Cramer has been investing in the stock market, and making money for himself and others, for almost three decades. This book will help you get in the mindset for putting money away and investing it.

The Professional's Guide To Modeling - Roger Talley
Our competition. I thought it was very good, very well written. Covers some stuff that our book doesn't and vice versa. Grab a copy.

Break Into Modeling For Under $20 - Judy Goss
Almost every modeling book looks down on "guys who pay to shoot pictures of you." While this book is no exception, it has better advice than some of the highbrow books I've seen, and lays out the fact that you can have a lucrative career without being one of a handful of supermodels.

Getting To Yes - Roger Fisher, William Ury
One of the best books on negotiation, first published in 1991. The best thing about education books is that more people have them on their shelves than have actually read them. Do yourself and your bank accounts a favor and read this one.

Trump-Style Negotiation - George H. Ross
I had to recommend this one, simply because of the popularity of The Apprentice. Cool book, but read *Getting To Yes* first.

Payment Processors

You should set up an account with at least two different companies, allowing you to accept payments digitally. While PayPal (owned by eBay) is the 800 lb gorilla of on-line payment processors, there are many people who have problems with using them, or even refuse to take or give payments via PayPal. Keep in mind, you'll want affiliate accounts, too, so you can make money by promoting pay-for-use web sites you appear on.

www.PayPal.com

www.2CheckOut.com

www.AlertPay.com

checkout.google.com

www.CCBill.com

AUTHOR BIOS

Antonio Giancarlo Perfetti (aka "Tony Perfect") has been shooting nude and nearly nude women since his mid-teens when he got the divorcee next door to pose in her swimsuit.

After several years as a social worker, he took up photography as a way to decompress after a hard day at the office. He still likes to visit exotic locations and shoot landscapes and animals, but more and more of his work is nudes, both artistic and erotic. He sees nothing wrong with combining all of the Creator's most beautiful work in one photo session.

Tony lives and works in the Tri-State area near NYC.

Scott Gardner is the founding member of Agile' Marketing Services, LLC. He shoots photos for press releases, but is no where near the artist that Tony is. He's been involved with writing and marketing for over 20 years.

Scott lives in a tiny town just north of Syracuse, NY.

Special Offer

You've read the book, and want even more information about Adult Internet Modeling? Great! We offer an on-line self-study program.

To learn more about it, we're offering a

FREE Video Seminar
(webinar)

to the first 137 people who visit the following link:

www.AdultModelingBook.com/vs

You've been good enough to buy our book, and we hope you've learned quite a bit about Adult Internet Modeling. For making it all the way to the end, we've put together several things to offer you as a

BONUS

❖ FREE Audio CD ($8.97 shipping and handling) with an interview of several models who have read and used the book to build themselves a better life as an Adult Internet Model.
❖ $10 OFF the companion workbook - a $25 dollar value for only $15. The workbook will help you:

❑ Develop Goals
❑ Develop Plan
❑ Create action steps to reach them

Visit

www.AdultModelingBook.com/store

And enter code BOOKBONUS when checking out.

Advanced Training

We're putting together a select group of successful models who will be traveling around the country and offering a seminar on advanced, in-depth training on the SAIM 9 Rules™ and the other chapters of our book.

To learn more about it, please visit

www.AdultModelingBook.com/at

If we're not visiting a city close to you in the near future, visit the web site and contact us about Advanced Training On-line!

www.ingramcontent.com/pod-product-compliance
Lightning Source LLC
Chambersburg PA
CBHW082107210326
41599CB00033B/6618